The Writing Tutor

by

Scott J. Warnock &
Stephen C. Zelnick

Edited by
James L. Marra & Mark T. Mattson

KENDALL/HUNT PUBLISHING COMPANY
4050 Westmark Drive   Dubuque, Iowa 52202

Copyright © by Mark Mattson, Steve Zelnick, James Mara

ISBN 0-7872-7478-X

Printed in the United States of America
10 9 8 7 6 5 4 3 2 1

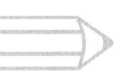

Table of Contents

Part Three: Top Twelve Problems

Part Four: Secrets of "A" Students

Appendix: Sample Papers

Preface

Guidebooks and handbooks on writing are abundantly available; still, students and their teachers tend not to use them. They seem overwhelming, to introductory students, and to many of their instructors, especially those without special training in rhetoric and grammar and deep experience in teaching writing. Though they are called handbooks, the user needs awfully big hands to grasp several hundred pages of detailed explanations offered in the specialized codes of experts.

The <u>Writing Tutor</u> simplifies writing instruction to the essentials, to provide students and their instructors a clear path to improved writing. We have asked ourselves, "What are the most common errors in student writing; where do they come from; and, what is the easiest advice for fixing them?"

The book is arranged in five parts:

- ✏ First Drafts
- ✏ Revising
- ✏ The Top Dozen Problems and How to Fix Them
- ✏ Secrets of "A" Students
- ✏ An Appendix, with Sample Essays

The book identifies each item clearly and provides explanations that avoid specialized language. Surprisingly, clear and simple explaining requires greater teaching experience than most handbooks use. The two authors of this book combine many years of teaching writing and training teachers of writing with deep experience in tutoring students on immediate problems.

There are already many excellent, more advanced books on writing. And students and instructors who develop a passion for the subject ought to go and study them. Here is a list of some of our favorites:

- ✏ Peter Elbow, <u>Writing With Power</u>
- ✏ Richard Lanham, <u>Revising Prose</u>
- ✏ Donald Murray, <u>A Writer Teaches Writing</u>
- ✏ William J. Strunk and E. B. White, <u>The Elements of Style</u>
- ✏ Joseph Williams, <u>Style: Ten Lessons in Clarity and Grace</u>
- ✏ William Zinsser, <u>On Writing Well</u>

Our little book, however, aims for the highest possible usefulness for beginners, both students and their teachers, drawing upon many years of experience of those who wrestle with the basic needs of writing students.

A Note to Students

Students complain that they don't see why they have to take all these writing courses. Not only are students required to take a basic course in writing, but it seems that several other courses, designated as writing intensive, also concentrate on writing. Most courses, not even about writing, assign papers and evaluate work on the basis of writing ability. Not only that, but some students seem to win favor and higher grades because they speak well and offer opinions and ask questions. Is it fair that "buttering up" the teacher counts so much?

There are two strong answers to this complaint. First, the only way anyone can estimate what you know and have learned is to read or listen to what you say. Your sentiment of knowledge—the feeling that you really do know something well—is worthless until you can express what you know clearly to someone else. Usually, the impression of mastery turns out to be an illusion. When you try to say what you think you know, it comes out wrong, sometimes pitifully wrong.

Education at the higher levels is about increasing precision and clarity. Having the general idea is not good enough as you climb the educational ladder. Education ratchets up the demands for explicit knowledge as you move from one class level to the next.

Putting your thoughts down on paper so that they make sense both to you and to a reader is an excellent way to discover what you do know and also what is still out of reach for you. Writing is a mode of discovery and of learning.

Want a second reason why all this writing is necessary? Look out at the world. Leaders across fields and professions may differ in hundreds of ways, but one quality they share is the ability to communicate effectively. In today's world—a world of information and selling ideas—people who speak and write effectively can rise to the top. They may not necessarily command vast commercial empires, but if they lack strong communication skills, they aren't going anywhere.

People find pleasure in listening to speakers and reading the words of writers who are confident and clear, people who can make difficult ideas intelligible and plan actions with clarity and purpose so that others will gladly follow. Presidents, corporate leaders, religious leaders, news analysts, military chiefs—all people prominent in public life are required to express themselves well. Those who command especially powerful communication skills have a good chance of becoming leaders. Those whose thoughts seem muddled and whose expression is uncertain and boring have an almost impossible climb to success.

Learning to write well is so important that the faculty who designed your curriculum have put writing instruction in as many places as it will fit. They have done so even though they know how hard it is for them to teach and how much extra work it is to assign and grade essays and provide useful instruction. They also have required this instruction because they believe these courses can make you a better writer. This book serves that goal for students and teacher alike.

A Note to Instructors

Teaching writing is no easy task. These days many people who have no special training are asked to teach writing as if it were something anyone who is well educated and a competent writer can do. However, most instructors faced with this obligation don't know what to do other than to encourage students to obey the rules and to circle the errors on student papers.

Some teachers in their desperation read grammar books to their students, and others stand at the blackboard labeling parts of speech.

Many conscientious instructors put in long hours marking up the margins of student papers with running commentary and then filling a page with close handwritten suggestions and evaluative comments. Most students then peek at the grade, stuff the returned paper deep into their book bag, and never even look at let alone read through the painstaking commentary their teachers have labored over.

With this book you are now equipped with many pieces of advice and several preliminary routines to start students into their essays. You may want to guide them through the early stages of their essays suggested in Part I, monitoring their progress day by day towards the first draft.

Many writing instructors are finding that the most efficient writing instruction is done through revision. The essays students typically submit are still groping towards a strong first draft. The paper doesn't yet have clearly indicated parts, the stance of the writer is far from firm, and the essay bears all the marks of uncertainty and messiness indicated in Part II.

A useful strategy is to

- ✏ mark up the errors,
- ✏ revise repeated errors (don't correct them all, but correct the first two instances and invite the student to correct the remaining ones of that particular error —you may want to asterisk the locations of that same error),
- ✏ discuss in marginal commentary opportunities for expanding the discussion, and
- ✏ offer a full assessment and a guide to revision in a summary comment.

The Re-submit Strategy

The important step is to require students to revise and re-submit their papers based upon the commentary and advice you have provided. This means that students have to read your comments with care and use them as a specific guide to revision.

The re-submit strategy of writing instruction allows you also to give the really low grades that poorly prepared essays deserve instead of the "happy face grades" students have come to expect. When the grade is low (and truthful), you can always encourage the student by observing that the grade on the re-submitted essay is the one you take seriously. Student evaluations may grumble that your grading is harsh but will then commend you for fairness for allowing revision.

Requiring students to submit the marked-up original along with the revision allows you to see whether the student really has been able to incorporate your instructions into the revised paper.

Some instructors require students to type out the summary comment from the original and staple it to the revised submission. Having the student copy over your remarks often means the comments hit home in detail.

The stance of the instructor with the re-submit strategy is much more rational. You can say:

- ✏ "It is my job to teach you how to produce a much better paper.
- ✏ I want you to do your best and to be able to achieve the grade, truthfully, that will make you happy.
- ✏ I don't want to be grading you for skills you brought into the course but for skills you are developing in this course.
- ✏ Most of all it is my job to teach you to revise thoughtfully and with care; that's what all good writers do."

Students sometimes complain about having to redo a paper they feel finished with. It may help to show them a piece of writing you are doing, all marked up, cut and pasted, with cross-outs and marginal replacement sentences. Revising is what writers do.

If your course includes several writing assignments, and it should, you may want to shift the revising burden progressively onto the students with each additional assignment. So,

- ✏ on the first paper you may choose not to grade the original submission at all but only the revision (a student can go from an "F" to an "A");
- ✏ on the second assignment, however, it is a good idea not to encourage students to submit an original that has not been revised at all. You may want to set a rule whereby the original paper receives a grade and the revision can increase only one grade level (from say a "C+" to a "B+"); and
- ✏ on the final assignment, there ought to be no re-submission opportunity; the submitted paper should have gone through the revision process now internalized by the student and not initiated by the instructor at all.

Writing instruction is really best done on actual pieces of student writing. Anything else is too abstract and too far from the student's needs. Working through revision techniques with students is an efficient and effective way to teach writing.

1 First Drafts

Everything Starts with The Assignment

Assignments almost always come from some classroom activity. Teachers like to link writing to lectures and discussions that follow reading assignments. So, it helps to review your notes and recall presentations you have heard before you tackle the assignment.

Often students overlook the information contained in the assignment itself and make the task all the more difficult. Let's take a typical assignment and break it down to find the information it contains:

> The Bill of Rights (the first ten amendments to the U.S. Constitution) was included to quiet the fears among representatives of the separate states that the newly formed government might overwhelm them and trample upon their rights. Identify three of these amendments that protect those rights and explain, with specific examples, the fears that some of the Founders must have had. Be sure to indicate the specific language that shows these concerns among the delegates who argued for these amendments.

This assignment is certainly complex, and you would surely be off on the wrong foot to think it says:

> Write an essay about the Bill of Rights.

You need to decide...

- ✏ which of these sentences provides information about context,
- ✏ which tells you what to do, and
- ✏ which provides specifications about how to do it.

Often the opening sentence or two are **_context_ _sentences_**. In this case...

> The Bill of Rights (the first ten amendments to the U.S. Constitution) was included to quiet the fears among representatives of the separate states that the newly formed government might overwhelm them and trample upon their rights.

The sentence which tells you what to do contains **command words:**

> **Identify** three of these amendments that protect those rights and **explain,** with specific examples, the fears that some of the Founders must have had.

The <u>specifications</u> appear primarily in the concluding sentence;

> Be sure to **indicate the specific language** that shows these concerns among the delegates who argued for these amendments.

Although in this case the comment in the previous sentence tells you what your teacher expects you to do.

Examine the following assignment with care, and identify the <u>context comments,</u> the <u>commands,</u> and the <u>specifications:</u>

> In the paper you write, choose carefully the data from the articles we have been studying in order to compare the roles of mothers in the period before World War Two with the roles of mothers in 1990. While economics may seem to answer all questions, technology also changed dramatically over this span of years, as did attitudes towards sexual behavior and towards children. Try to include what seem to you the most important data and explain why the data you choose is the most important.

> ✏ So, what are you supposed to do? *(Commands)*
> ✏ What are you to assume? *(Context)*
> ✏ What should you absolutely not fail to include *(Specifications)*

Instructors: You may want to construct topics in the subject of the course and have students practice identifying commands, context, and specifications. Not only is this good preparation for the papers you are assigning, but it is also an excellent opportunity to review course material.

Questions to Ask

Usually, teachers provide all the specifics you will need to understand the writing assignment. However, when the teacher doesn't, go ahead and ask. The teacher will appreciate the better papers that will result, and your classmates will thank you. You should ask the following questions

- ✏ Am I permitted to use "I" in this essay?
- ✏ Am I allowed to use sources?
- ✏ Am I required to use sources, and, if so, are there specific sources that I must use (your class textbook, for instance)?
- ✏ What form do I use to cite my sources?
- ✏ Who is the audience of the assignment?
- ✏ How long should the assignment be?
- ✏ Should I have a title?
- ✏ When is the due date?
- ✏ Will I get a chance to revise this essay?

Audience

Everything written is written for some reader or group of readers. Student writers often assume that the reader must be the teacher. Nothing could be worse!

After all, the teacher knows everything you are going to be writing about. It is highly unlikely that you will be able to teach her anything about what she has spent years mastering. With this sort of reader, all you can hope for is not to embarrass yourself too badly.

In fact, the very word "author" assumes that the writer has authority, is an expert, the very person you would go to for an explanation. If you imagine you are writing for the teacher, who is an expert, then how can you be an author?

Better to provide yourself another reader entirely, one who does not know more than you. Imagine a reader who knows enough less than you so that you become the expert. Here are some possibilities:

- ✏ You are writing for a student in your class who missed the class session where this particular material was discussed. This student comes to you and asks: "Can you explain X?" or "How would I go about comparing Y with Z?"
- ✏ You are writing for your younger brother who is in high school and has received the assignment (that in reality you just received from your teacher).
- ✏ It is Spring break and your cousin, who attends another college, asks you to explain what the assignment asks you to explain.

In each case, you are the authority, and your reader needs your careful explanation to understand the assigned topic.

This approach is particularly appropriate because academic writing, at its best, is much like good teaching. Even for academic readers who know a great deal, writing conventions assume careful explanation and slow and careful gathering of evidence and arguments to persuade and instruct the reader. By assuming the authoritative role you are more likely to develop your explanations with patience and care. In the process, you may also prove to yourself that you know what you are talking about.

All this is far more difficult if you are writing for the teacher, a reader who knows everything and doesn't need your explanations.

Roles of the Author

Who are you when you write? Students experience a strange feeling when they find themselves cast as writers. Suddenly, you are no longer just little you; instead you are being asked to become someone more formal, more significant, more public.

We could become profoundly psychological about this transformation, but the easiest way is to think about the roles you will play as a writer. In a school setting, we can assign these roles as follows: the host, the teacher, and the lawyer.

1. The Host

All writers are obligated to be friendly towards their readers. Readers are guests, so to speak, in your paper. As author, you have already spent several days considering your topic and developing your views. You reader, however, has just come upon what you have written and needs to

- ✏ warm to the topic,
- ✏ get in step with your thinking,
- ✏ understand what the issues are,
- ✏ see where the problems are with those issues,
- ✏ know in what direction some solution may lie, and
- ✏ ponder why these matters are important in the first place.

A good host settles his guest comfortably by anticipating her needs and finding ways to satisfy them. Suppose a stranger comes to dinner at your house. She rings the bell and enters into your foyer. You as host must greet her, introduce her to other guests, take her coat, show her a bit of the house. At dinner it would be kind and polite to describe the courses of the meal so your guest will know what and how much to eat in each course and how to leave room for dessert. Of course, you would introduce this stranger to other guests, especially those with whom she had something in common.

As a writer you have to show this same consideration for your reader's needs. This means you must

- ✏ offer an introduction that settles your reader into the issues and problems,
- ✏ provide something of a map of your discussion and indicate **transitions** clearly, and
- ✏ whenever you use a new word or introduce a new concept or a new set of facts your reader likely will not know, you should stop the momentum of your argument to explain.

Remarkably, the standard you must reach for is to present a paper that will never force the reader to stop in confusion and re-read what came before. You must be **Reader-Friendly**. You want your reader never to have to scratch his head, feel lost, or think he's stupid.

Think of your own needs as a reader and how annoyed you are to be swamped by something you are trying to understand. Follow here the golden rule: do for your reader what you as a reader would wish to be done for you.

Think of the best teacher you ever had, the teacher who seemed always to know when you were confused and stopped to explain herself until you could see what she had in mind. That's what you have to do as a writer.

2. The Teacher

A good writer in the school setting has to emulate good teaching. The task of presenting information, developing concepts, and creating new ways to view things is what school writing is all about.

The writer must, therefore, explain patiently and with care to a reader who does not yet understand what you have to say. As with the good host, the good teacher must anticipate the difficulties his reader will have:

- What in the material is not well known and therefore must be explained with care; and when, on the other hand, can you just keep going because the reader already knows the material well (and will be insulted if you stop to explain it)?
- Where, in the concept, is the hard part, the notion that will at first seem strange, or impossible, or even ridiculous to your reader?
- When is the view you are developing obvious and needs no explanation, and when is it strange and difficult and needs all your powers of explanation to be understood by your reader?

3. The Lawyer

The third role you have to assume when writing a school paper is that of the lawyer. You will be claiming that certain things are true and other things are untrue. Just how do you know these things? What information allows you to make the claims you do? How can you validate that information? How can you prove it?

Your reader has a right to know how you know what you claim to know. What guarantees that what you claim is true?

Quoting from authoritative sources is probably the best way to satisfy this requirement for your reader. Presenting data, and sources of those data, provides strength to your argument; but beyond that, it is the only way your reader can know that she should take you seriously and come to the conclusions you wish her to.

The three roles—host, teacher, lawyer—provide a good list to help your instructor think about where your essay has succeeded and where it has failed. It is, therefore, a useful checklist for you when you are polishing and revising your paper for submission.

Developing Perspectives

What you write ought to make a difference, or why write (other than, of course, to fulfill the assignment)? Discovering a purpose for your essay will often make the difference between a flat performance and a piece of writing that would capture the attention of your imagined reader (and does capture the attention of your real reader, your teacher).

An excellent place to start is by asking yourself what your imagined reader already knows about the subject and what he thinks.

For example, imagine the student who missed the excellent lecture on the divisions among the Founding Fathers at the Convention which agreed upon the U.S. Constitution. He may very likely think that

- in Constitutional times people were much more agreeable than they are today, or that
- because they are our elders, they were wise and purely rational, or that
- the U.S. Constitution is a mess of platitudes, or full of mostly "lawyer talk" that has no bearing on life as lived.

These confused notions may be the same ones you had before the class discussion taught you otherwise.

Armed with these three "confusions" that you have good reason to expect in your reader, you now have a much better sense of what your task is as a writer. In clarifying these confusion, you have discovered the purpose for your essay. When you are done with your reader, he will have moved from confusion to much greater clarity, just as you did a week or two ago in class.

Differentiations

Thinking your way into a map or outline of the essay you are beginning to write can be an ordeal. Sometimes the topic at the center of the assignment seems like a jungle of tangled notions and sometimes, and even worse, the topic seems to be so easily settled you can't imagine how an essay can come from it.

Here are four ways to attack this problem.

1. Definitions

One major purpose for essays is to make useful distinctions between closely related concepts. Academics have worked hard at this all the way back to Socrates, who was always helping his fellow citizens to think clearly and use words well.

You may be asked in an assignment to distinguish between a "good character" in a story and a character who possesses a "good character." Or, you may have to clarify the distinction between a person who acts justly by obeying the law and another who follows justice by disobeying the law in order to obey a higher law, superior to the laws human beings make.

Often what seems clear is not clear at all. Is a democratic state one in which every issue is put to a popular vote and the majority rules, or one which has built in restrictions so that the majority cannot harm a minority or trample upon its rights?

2. Comparison/Contrast

Another kind of differentiation requires comparing and contrasting two related but distinct entities. For example, basketball and soccer are both team sports, but discovering the essential differences between them can reveal the nature of each in surprising ways. "Social democracy" and "liberal democracy" both make claims for being democratic, but the differences between these two social systems are important to explore. Classical music and Romantic music are both European musical styles each employing many similar types of ensembles, yet the differences can be dramatically revealed by a contrasting that begins with comparison.

Comparison and contrast essays explore topics by shifting between similarities and differences. The formal arrangement of comparison/contrast essays usually follow one of two patterns:

Form I: Form I goes through each sport (basketball, and then soccer) point by point, one at a time, and doing most of the comparing and contrasting in the sport presented second.

So, for example, you would notice that basketball can depend upon team strategy, but that sometimes with a superior player on the team, teamwork suffers. You would mention that scoring is frequent in basketball. You would observe that basketball requires height and strength. And finally, you might comment that basketball requires more brains than most people suppose.

Soccer is similar in some ways and very different in others. With more than twice the number of people on a much larger field, soccer may employ much more strategy, and it is unlikely a single superior player can dominate. Scoring seems almost never to happen, and many people find soccer difficult to watch as a result. Soccer, unlike basketball, can be played by average sized players and small players often excel; stamina is most important. And soccer players must always be thinking about where the game is and where they are in the game.

In Form I Comparison-Contrast, you go through each sport, point by point.

Form II: Form II is organized by topic, first with one sport and then with the other. You would discuss team elements, first in basketball then in soccer. Your next paragraph would present the differences in

19

scoring frequency and what difference that makes. The third discusses the size, strength and speed of the athletes. And the fourth compares the different kinds of intelligence in each sport.

Neither form is more correct than the other. It depends on the material and the needs of the audience. But it helps to know how to structure this basic type of differentiation essay.

3. Argumentation

Argumentation essays require a fair treatment of both, or multiple sides of an issue. We are accustomed in the "real" world to making arguments only on one side. The academic tradition, however, is supposed to be a search for truth rather than for mere victory in the argument. Your teacher will respond very positively if your argument essay spends time making the case for opposing sides and only then arguing for the superiority of one side over another (or others).

Suppose you are asked to discuss whether students should be treated as customers, as young persons, or as apprentices. There surely is a case for each of these positions, and it would show significant thoughtlessness to deny it.

Suppose you are to argue the merits of the death penalty, whether TV programming should be regulated to shield youngsters from dangerous materials, whether co-ed residence halls are a good idea...and so on. In each case you want to make clear that you are aware of the opposing arguments and that you have considered each seriously.

The position you end up arguing for will be more believable once it is clear that you are well aware of the objections on the other side, have considered them sensibly, and found good reasons for rejecting them.

Argumentation essays always require that you display broad knowledge of your subject and good judgment in reaching your conclusion.

4. Analysis

Students often are stumped because there doesn't seem much to say. A "bottom-line" conclusion—"this is good; that is bad"—is all that seems worth saying.

For example, if you were asked to write a paper on Adam Smith's discussion of free trade versus tariffs, it would be obvious that Smith favors free trade over trade restrictions. You are required, however, to write 1,000 words and all you can generate is: "In his monumental work <u>The Wealth of Nations</u> (1776) the great Scottish economist, Adam Smith, comes out in favor of free trade over trade restrictions." That's only twenty-five words. So, now what?

One move is to ask why nations would favor trade restrictions in the first place (favorable balance of trade, protecting jobs, sheltering infant industries from competition, etc.). Another move would ask what different forms these restriction take (special licenses, high taxes on imports, bans on imports, etc.). Now you have two good paragraphs just on the expanded definitions of trade restrictions.

Turning to free trade, you might ask exactly who benefits from free trade and how. Enumerating the list generates the remainder of your essay. You would discover that free trade is

- good for consumers (many imports and domestic products competing for the consumer's dollar and competing also for quality recognition);
- good also for merchants of various kinds (obviously importers will have more business activity in an unrestricted market, but exporters will also benefit since they will not face retaliatory tariffs from other nations);
- good also for investors and banks since there is expanded need for investing in many ventures abroad;
- good for manufacturers who also benefit since they now have access to many different national markets (they will have to compete of course, but that means that many more manufacturers are allowed into the game); and
- good for workers who benefit because expanded business activity means more jobs (although a particular industry may be pressured out of existence, many more will spring up).

You might expand the list even further by noting that

- ✏ national economies will flourish (at least Smith thinks so) because there will be more jobs, more goods of better quality and in greater variety at a cheaper price, more investment opportunity, and so on;
- ✏ a global marketplace brings goods from one part of the world to another (coconuts to Norway; fine French wines to India; Argentinean beef to Italy; and so on) that otherwise would never be available; and finally
- ✏ a world at economic peace instead of endless aggressive restrictions is Smith's ultimate hope for free trade.

Now look at all there is to talk about when you ask some very simple questions. What are the parts of this definition? Good for whom? Now you will find it difficult to write the essay in only one thousand words. Analysis, or breaking the subject down into parts, helps you generate ideas and ultimately a rich full essay.

Using Sources

Most writing courses depend upon readings to supply source materials for writing assignments. Teachers want to see whether students can coordinate their reading, with discussion (speaking and listening), and writing.

Assigned topics for writing may call upon general outlooks from the readings, but inevitably teachers expect quotations from the readings to appear in your essay. Some assignments may even specify the number of quotations or even a word count requirement for quotations.

You should remember that quotations are not simply decorative. Using quotations

- ✏ means that you are a person who consults informed materials, a thoughtful person who has not simply pulled stuff out of the air or merely depended upon your own limited experience; and
- ✏ lends weight and authority to the point you are making if the quotation is from a noted thinker.

Teachers separate veteran writers from rookies by the way students use quotations. New writers tend to drop an entire haystack of words into their essays, using large block quotes and in effect, asking the reader to pick out the valuable parts. Practiced writers do this careful choosing for the reader and zero in on the exact sentence or even few words that make the point precisely. Also, the writer must introduce the quotation, which cannot speak for itself. Your job is to alert your reader so that she knows just how the quote fits your discussion (see Part 3 for examples).

In preparing your paper, mark passages in the readings that you may use. Create an inventory list of these passages so you know what you have available. If you have the time, copy the passages out on note cards so that the passages themselves are readily available.

Warning: Quotations carry the greatest danger for misspelling, dropped punctuation, and omitted words. These errors may occur because the passage has been transcribed, or it may be that because these words are not yours you don't have full control of them. Be sure to check the quotation in your paper against the original passage.

Plagiarism

One of the worst and most dangerous offenses you can be charged with in school is plagiarism. If you submit work that includes plagiarized material, your teacher will certainly fail that assignment. You may fail the course. You may even be brought before a Disciplinary Board for punishment (and possible expulsion) if your plagiarism is persistent.

In general, you have committed plagiarism when you present as your own work writing or ideas that belong to someone else. The source may be a book, magazine, another student, or the internet.

The test for whether an idea needs to be attributed to someone else is whether it is in any way unusual or original:

> ✏ If the source you are using mentions that there are fifty-two weeks in a year, you don't need to attribute (give the source for) that since everyone knows it.

- If the source mentions that the outer planets serve the function of capturing and diverting asteroids from the inner planets of the solar system, you must attribute this unusual idea to its source.
- But suppose the source offers the calculation of the speed at which the earth travels around the sun? Anyone can do that calculation easily, and it is a number well known to those who bother about astronomy. Here, it would depend on what level the course is and who the intended reader is supposed to be.

Students are caught plagiarizing more than you would think. It isn't that your teacher knows every word on this subject that has ever been written, but teachers can tell the difference between student writing and professional writing. Weak students are routinely caught plagiarizing because the gap between what they write in class and what they submit for out-of-class work is so wide. This goes for idea content, too. When the student who can never seem to answer an in-class question suddenly becomes brilliant on paper, teachers become especially alert to fraud.

Plagiarized papers, especially those lifted directly from the internet, are immediately suspect because their approach does not match the assignment or the teacher's emphases in class discussion. Internet plagiarism is especially risky because once teachers become suspicious, they can trace the paper through word chain searches.

While this is not the place for a long discussion of plagiarism, we will mention a few points:

- Use sources responsibly. This issue has become more and more prevalent with the use of Web and internet sources, which writers often think they can use without citing. Basically, use the same guidelines for computer sources that you use for print sources.
- It doesn't matter how many times you cite a source in a paper, you must cite each separate use.
- If the idea is not yours, cite it. And it doesn't matter if you use a direct quote or a paraphrase.

Starting Out

Most writers report difficulty starting the actual writing. Once you have selected the assignment and broken down its parts so you know what you are to do, you enter the twilight world of puttering around and delaying getting down to work.

Many writers report evasive action. They wash dishes, clean bathtubs, dust Venetian blinds, wash their cars, iron loads of wash. Oddly, while this evasive hyper-activity goes on, your mind often is working quietly on the thoughts that support the essay you will soon be writing. If you pay attention to this automatic and mysterious mind activity, you may even notice sentences forming in the undercurrent of your mind.

Don't panic. This is weird but quite normal.

Some writers in the second phase of preparation grab the task directly and attempt to form an outline of the essay. This is also recommended, but please remember that the outline can only be a rough guide since you don't know yet what you will be saying exactly. If you outline too decisively, you block the flow of ideas that will stream out as you settle into writing.

Many other writers find outlining too confining and prefer, surprisingly enough, to start writing before they know where they are going. Many writers and people who study writing report that loosening the flow of words comes before intentional writing, where you know more precisely what you want to say and how you want to say it.

Here are a few routines to loosen your word flow:

Timed Free Writing

Set yourself a time limit—say, three minutes. With your topic in mind, just begin writing and see what flows out of your pencil (pencil on paper usually helps because it allows you to think that this product is less formidable, more of a playful draft). The only other rule is that you cannot pause or stop writing; press on.

At three minutes, stop and catch your breath. Now, have a look at what you wrote and pick out the most important thought.

Cycles

Start another timed writing with the thought (or word) that strikes you as most important (or explosive, or odd, or mysterious). Write for another three minutes, without pause. Now, review this second round and repeat another cycle.

At this point, you have written for a mere ten minutes. However, you should find that something unexpected has happened. Thoughts in sentences are beginning to flow in your mind, and you are now ready to begin a first draft.

Probing Questions

Other writers need more logical ways to start and find ways to analyze their topic by subjecting it to a series of clarifying questions:

Suppose you are writing about mandatory school uniforms—

- Who supports this proposal; who opposes it?
- How did this become an issue?
- Has this policy been attempted? With what results?
- What can it accomplish? What problems will it begin?
- How will it help students? Their parents? Their teachers?
- How will it harm students? Their parents? Their teachers?
- What have supporters argued? What have opponents argued?
- Is it for everybody or only certain kind of schools? What kinds?
- Does this policy look different to boys/girls? rich/poor? ethnic/mainstream? city/suburb? arts/practical? etc.
- Is this likely to be adopted?

A list like this helps you work your way into the issue and to gather what you know about it. It is a way to search your topic and your thoughts and data and begin to organize your themes (that is, your ideas about the topic). Of course, as you write your answers to these prompts, you will also be loosening your flow of words.

Theme Cards

You may want to mark these themes (or thoughts) as they begin to become clearer to you through this preliminary thinking. One way to proceed is to use note cards (3x5 will do) to jot down each thought as it occurs to you. These themes will not necessarily be in any order, but once you know more about what you have to say, you can order these note cards by sorting them into categories. These categories will become sections of your essay. The note cards might also begin to suggest the order of your discussion. If you could not accomplish an outline earlier, you should be able to construct one now with some authority.

Any one of these strategies for starting out may work for you. The point is to warm to the task and work with the freedom of not yet absolutely knowing what is on your mind. If you can manage not to pressure yourself too hard in these preliminary games, you should find yourself relaxing into writing the first draft. Once words and ideas start flowing, writing the draft should be much easier. In writing, as in so much else, giving yourself time to play, to start the task in a way that seems not quite for real, allows you to get on into the phase when it is real. If you are time conscious, notice that these loosening up exercises should not take more than a half-hour, and many writers find that getting lost in these games is a more efficient use of their time than sulking. And, after all, how many dishes can you wash until you have to face the terrors of the blank page? This way, you have already begun writing and focusing your thoughts.

2 Revising

Introduction

All writers expect to revise what they write. The sentences you are reading looked different when this section of the book was first written out. In fact, this introduction was not listed in the original plan, but the need for it became clear when we reviewed the manuscript. We did not, however, think we had failed in not thinking to write this introduction. Instead, we were happy to discover the need for going back and getting it right.

Most revision, you will find, takes you right back to Part I and especially to the concerns for mapping out your discussion sensibly and fully and serving your reader's needs well.

You should expect that your instructor will offer suggestions about organization and clarity on your first drafts. However, if your instructor does not provide you an opportunity to re-submit your work, you should take it upon yourself to take a hard look at your draft before you submit it. Part I provides you a first-rate checklist for many of the big issues.

What follows in this section on revision focuses upon style issues—in brief, how your paper reads. Writing experts have long noticed that early drafts at all levels of skill share certain characteristics. These "errors" come primarily from uncertainty and haste, two "problems" that writers, even professional writers, cannot avoid with first drafts. The question is never whether what you write out the first time is going to be perfect or not, but whether you are willing to work on your early drafts to make them good.

Revising for Style

An old story goes that a man once wrote a long letter to his friend and apologized at the close of the letter. He wrote: "I am sorry to have written such a long letter, but I did not have time to write a shorter one."

This remark seems contradictory at first, but for those of us who write, it makes perfect sense. A first draft is almost always a lumpy thing, full of repetition and wasted words. Most of what you read—

and these days hear—in the media has been carefully crafted and cost the author or some editor hard sweat to make the words go right. To make remarks seem effortless usually requires great effort.

Why is this? Normally we think that what we write should emerge as a photograph of finished thoughts sitting inside our heads. When this fails to happen, students feel something is wrong with them. The truth is, however, that producing finished work worth anything requires a process of revision often requiring numerous drafts. The manuscripts of famous speeches and time-honored works of literature always show sentences dropped, words crossed out and replaced with new ones, added material squeezed into the margins, and even more radical cuts and pastes.

A moment's thought about how words get on paper helps explain why this is all perfectly natural. Early drafts are usually explorations for the writer:

- ✏ What do I know and think about this?
- ✏ What can I assert with confidence? And what is merely comfortable speculation?
- ✏ What do I really believe and feel about this?
- ✏ What does my reader know, think, feel, believe about this?
- ✏ What is the best way to say this?
- ✏ And much more.

This perfectly natural uncertainty in a first draft or even several early drafts leaves its mark on what we write. We should expect the following marks of uncertainty in early drafts.

Repetition

First drafts will likely be full of repetition. The writer, not knowing exactly what to say or how to say it, repeats the same idea several ways. As writers, we need to see how to put the idea and how it looks settling into other ideas to which it is related. We need to find the right words for it. And so we say the same thing several times in different ways.

Example:

> "Sports heroes carry a public responsibility they never chose
> and probably do not even want. They have placed upon
> them the burden of being a hero to young people, who look
> up to them to learn what it means to excel and compete at
> the highest level of ones talents. Youngsters look upon their
> sports heroes for a model they can use to imagine themselves
> as winners in life. Youngsters see their sports heroes as peo-
> ple far above the abilities they generally witness in the peo-
> ple around them, a total dedication to what they are doing
> as well as remarkable abilities and careful training. The train-
> ing of a world-class athlete brings out the athlete's native tal-
> ents to a level of rare perfection. Where else will a young
> man or woman get to see the rare combination of natural
> talent, drive to perfection, and careful sharpening of those
> talents? The sports hero presents to view a level of perfection
> one doesn't often see in life."

If you read this example carefully, you will see that it repeats two essential ideas two or three times. The writer is groping towards these essential ideas by expressing them in several ways. The writer, for example, shifts perspective from the athlete to the youngster observing the athlete. Which way says it best? The writer is groping towards a list of three features the athlete exemplifies and has not quite settled into this idea but is moving closer.

In a first draft, this sort of repetition is just fine, but in the revision the writer will have to choose exactly what he wants to say. Perhaps it will read something like this:

> "Sports heroes carry a burden they never meant to assume.
> Youngsters look up to them because athletes represent some-
> thing rare in life, the combination of magnificent natural tal-
> ent, personal dedication, and extraordinary training. Where
> else in life will a young man or woman see perfection dis-
> played so openly? Where else can the young find a model for
> their own dreams of perfection?"

The revision is much cleaner, and its parts are far better coordinated. The point, however, is that most writers need to write the first draft before they can attain the better version. It helps to know that repetition, though normal and useful, is a characteristic of first drafts you can expect to find and a target for revision.

Assertions

Oddly, the more uncertain we are, the more likely we are to use <u>certainty words.</u> When we say

- "I believe"
- "I feel"
- "certainly"
- "it is clear that"

it is almost always because we doubt what we are saying, don't feel comfortable about it, are not certain, and are in a fog. We try to make ourselves feel certain by using terms of certainty. Using the word "Truly" may be more of a prayer than an assertion—it says, "I hope this is true." The more we use certainty words, the more we raise questions about what we assert, and somewhere along the route of revision, we will have to decide what we really do believe, think, feel and propose with certainty. When we reach that point, we can drop the "certainty words" and simply write what we think.

Example:

"**<u>Obviously,</u>** politicians are in politics only to advance their own wealth, power, and reputation, rather than to do the public any good. **I <u>believe</u>** that people who choose to run for public office have to have a large measure of arrogance and self-esteem. They are **<u>truly</u>** doing it only for their own good. **<u>Certainly,</u>** no one would choose to go through all the torment of running for office if he or she was not an egomaniac of some sort. **It <u>is</u> <u>clear</u>** that politicians are in it only to make themselves famous, rich, and powerful. **<u>Sure,</u>** there are some exceptions, but **I <u>feel</u> <u>strongly</u>** that these exceptions are so rare that they only go to prove how **<u>true</u>** the opposite is for politicians generally."

This example ought to make you nervous. All those certainty words only point up how unsure the writer is. They signal to the reader the opposite of what they say. Instead of evidence, example, illustration, or argumentation, all we get is aggressive assurances. Certainty words say "I better do some reading and find some evidence; I could be wrong."

What do you do when the certainty words pile up in a first draft? Look for the hard evidence or strong example that will allow you to make your assertion without these slippery words. In a first draft, they are telling you "this is a place in my discussion where I need to do more work."

Back-loaded Sentences

One sure sign of uncertainty is the patter we put early in our sentences to smooth the way to expressing our assertions. In a back-loaded sentence, what is most important comes at the end while the beginnings of our sentences are packed with words that don't do much. Early drafts are full of this patter. One reason we find verbiage cluttering up the early parts of our sentences is that

- ✏ in first drafts we write on even when we are thinking what we want to say. The pencil moves on with something like a mind of its own;
- ✏ we are not sure what we want to say, so we would rather not come right out with it just yet; and finally
- ✏ these sentences sound so learned and professorial, as if they were the product of deliberate consideration.

Example:

"Many people have come to feel after reviewing the matter fully and communing deeply with their best selves and conferring with those people knowledgeable in such matters that war is hell."

This example exaggerates, but you will find something like it in your first draft, every time. War, like writing, is hell.

33

You might note that the early part of this sentence is full of material about the conditions of knowledge for this assertion. Often you do need these qualifying comments that clog the opening of your sentences; a simple solution is to front-load your revised sentence.

Example:

> "Upon reviewing all his carefully notated data on his observations of the stars surrounding the planet Jupiter, **Galileo was prepared to venture a more certain hypothesis.** If the apparent stars appeared in a straight line across the face of Jupiter, **they might not be stars at all.** Once he had imagined seeing these sources of light from a different perspective entirely, **Galileo was able to recognize that they were moons orbiting Jupiter.** When he had fully thought through the data he had compiled in his notebooks, **Galileo announced his shocking findings to the scientific world.** Even for modern people to whom modern science is common and familiar, **Galileo continues to appear brave and decisive."**

Which of these five sentences would you front-load?

Suppressed Agency

In our uncertainty, we may not want to assign responsibility. The most famous example is the modern politician's comment "Mistakes were made." Who made the mistake; who did what? Usually, the early draft sentence signals this confusion by "there are..." sentences.

Example:

> "There are many ways in which Charles Dickens, the author of <u>Hard Times</u>, is seen to be in opposition to the industrial practices which existed in mid-Victorian England."

The solution here is to put the doer of the action in the agency position of the sentence. Or, to say it more simply, since Charles Dickens does the action, we can clarify the sentence by putting him first:

Revised:

> "Charles Dickens, the author of <u>Hard Times</u>, opposed the industrial practices of Mid-Victorian England."

Grammar doesn't demand this. However, our minds tend to think-- "who did what?" So, putting Dickens first in the sentence allows us to recognize him as the subject and also the doer (agent) of the action.

In the same manner, placing the agent **(Dickens)** close to the verb **(opposed)** satisfies our need to know "who did what."

Teachers talk about another problem of suppressed agency as **(a) Passive and (b) Active** Construction.

a. Passive Construction

Example:

> "Many industrial workers were encouraged to involve them-selves in radical union activity by skilled organizers who hated the cruelty and injustice of mid-Victorian capitalism."

In this sentence, the grammatical subject ("industrial workers") are not the doers of the action ("skilled organizers" are). We can under-stand the sentence pretty well, but it would have more force and greater clarity if we put the agents in the subject position (changed from passive to active construction).

b. Active Construction

Example:

> "Skilled union organizers, who hated the cruelty and injus-tice of mid-Victorian England, encouraged industrial workers to participate in radical union activity."

Now the actors are in the subject position, and the sentence satis-fies our need for "who did what."

Burying the Verb

Good verbs assert vividly; so when we are uncertain, verbs suffer. They suffer in several ways:

a. Weak Verbs

For example, a common fault in student essays results from the use of the verb "states."

"Jefferson states that all men are created equal."

True enough, but the word "states" is too general and lacks punch. In fact, Jefferson

- ✏ "declares" (it is a declaration of independence, after all);
- ✏ "proclaims"
- ✏ "asserts"
- ✏ "announces"
- ✏ "testifies"
- ✏ and on and on.

"States" tells us that he utters this thought, somehow or other. The energetic verbs tell us just how he utters them; they communicate something forceful in the place of something bland. Verbs should sing and sting!

Example:

"The U.S. Supreme Court deals with the most important judicial cases."

The all-purpose and empty verb "deals with" is the sort of verb first drafts love. "Deals with" works like a marker; it say "I need a verb here, but I am still trying to figure out what I want to say, and I will return later and figure out what that verb ought to be." "Deals with" says "has something to do with;" it couldn't be more vague.

Revised:

"The U.S. Supreme Court decides the most important judicial cases."

"Involves" is another favorite place holder verb in first drafts.

Example:

"Democracy involves a well-informed electorate."
"Writing involves hard work."

Revised:

"Democracy depends upon a well-informed electorate."
"Writing fails without hard work."

b. Verbs in Disguise

We are all children of a bureaucratic age; and we have become accustomed to official prose. We find it more comfortable to say that

"Dickens is in opposition" than to say
"Dickens opposes."

The first sounds more careful and learned and complex. And suppose someone knows of an instance where Dickens did not oppose? This way, we can say something and not quite say it at the same time. But Dickens did oppose industrial practices and did so vividly in Hard Times. So, not to say that straight up is to tell a lie and confuse the reader.

The most familiar disguise has the verb dressed up like a noun and introduced by some form of the verb "to be"—"is," "are," "was," "were," and so on.

Example:

"The homeless man is in need of something to eat."

Revised:

"The homeless man needs something to eat."

c. Verbs in Sequence

Example:

"Some words serve to mask our uncertainty."
"Some words help to mask our uncertainty."
"Some words work to mask our uncertainty."

Now, which of the two verbs "serve" or "mask" says something? In fact, "serve to" adds nothing but words and bogus loftiness to this sentence.

Revised:

> "Some words mask our uncertainty."

Example:

> "The new residence hall will assist in providing more living space for students on campus."

Revised:

> "The new residence hall will provide more living space for students on campus."

d. Familiar Servants

Little verbs—

- ✏ "get"
- ✏ "put"
- ✏ "make"

like micro-organisms, invade our sentences and rob verbs of their energy.

- ✏ Do people "get married" or do they "marry"?
- ✏ Are two pieces "put together" or are they "attached?"
- ✏ Is something "made better" or "improved"?

In each cases, the little verb keeps things general and flat.

Example:

> "Adding that topic will only make the assignment more complicated."

Revised:

> "Adding that topic will only complicate the assignment."

Example:

> "We should put that discussion aside until all members are present."

Revised:

> "We should postpone that discussion until all members are present."

When we write quickly, we may not find the word we need. When revising, look for those "little verbs" and see whether you can replace them.

Words for Existence

We waste words to establish the existence of what we are discussing. These tags are like hiccups; they are reflexes, in this case of the pen and not the esophagus.

Example:

> "Dickens opposed the industrial practices, which existed at that time in mid-Victorian England."

Revised:

> "Dickens opposed the industrial practices of mid-Victorian England."

We already know that they existed at that time. Dickens would not have opposed them if they did not exist; and since these practices belonged to the mid-Victorian period, they were of that time.

This is all so silly, but we use these tags all the time. They fill the page, an attractive consideration when we feel challenged by a length requirement. They also extend the sentence, which offers the illusion of deep thinking.

Example:

> "Tyrannosaurus Rex, of the Jurassic period, was the mightiest creature that existed in that time period."

Revised:

> "Tyrannosaurus Rex was the mightiest creature of the Jurassic Period."

Adverbs be Gone!

Adverbs, another form of uncertainty words, sometimes serve as intensifiers to mask our uncertainty. "Very" often means "sort of" when we look closely; and "clearly" usually means "I'm not sure." "Always" can mean "sometimes" or maybe "not at all." "Really" has become suspect; when we have to write it, all is lost.

Example:

> "When I met his mother, she seemed really strange."

Revised:

> "When I met his mother, she seemed strange."

Now, isn't it odd that the sentence without "really" is more forceful? As with so much else in writing, less is more.

a. Multiple adverbs

Example:

> "A lot of people don't enjoy reading newspapers."

Revised:

> "Many people don't enjoy reading newspapers."

Example:

> "A lot of the time, teachers actually don't know exactly what they want."

Revised:

> "Often, teachers don't know what they want."

Multiple adverbs are fine in seventh grade writing but not in more mature prose.

Misplaced Modifiers

When we race along producing our first draft, a chunk of the sentence may end up in the wrong place. We know what we had in mind, but the sentence says something else.

Example:

"There is a picture of my last wife up on the wall."
(What was she doing up there when they took her picture?)

Or was it

"Up on the wall, there is a picture of my last wife."

Example:

"After the explosion, he decided only to bury the dead cat."
(Instead of dissecting it?)

Revised:

"After the explosion, he decided to bury only the dead cat."

Dangling modifiers can often be the most embarrassing modifier errors.

"Driving at excessive speed, the tree put a serious dent in my left bumper." (What a clever tree!)

The doer (agent) of the action must follow immediately after the modifying phrase.

"Driving at excessive speed, my daughter managed to put a serious dent in my bumper when she drove into a tree."

Example:

"Stolen yesterday, my grandmother found her car in ditch."
(Always lock your grandmother when you park her in a dangerous neighborhood!)

Dangling modifiers are very funny—when someone else writes them.

41

Sentence Variety

Unfortunately, with all the other things student writers have to think about, they have to think about music, too. Writing imitates voice, and if you are not careful you can fall into a deadly drone that invites your reader to sleep. One way to avoid the droning voice is to focus upon sentence length and variety.

Early drafts often fall into a dreary pattern—every sentence 11-17 words long, and with simple subject-verb-object construction. This happens especially with student papers because the student fears writing more complex sentences, where punctuation and coordination become problems, where the subject and verb are not always close by, and where the pronoun and antecedent may lose sight of one another. In other words, students write short to stay safe.

A good writing instructor should encourage students to try bold and unfamiliar sentence forms, to mix short and long sentences, to move the subject and verb into different positions from sentence to sentence, and reward the student who makes some mistakes but is trying to acquire a more mature style.

Example:

"Baby sentences won't do when you are writing an essay (10). Readers will find them boring, even though they are easy to follow (12). Nevertheless, many student writers choose to write short sentences feeling they are safe (13). You can avoid making mistakes when writing short sentences (9). Short sentences are easy to punctuate because they usually have only one or two clauses (15). Short sentences will usually help you avoid subject-verb agreement problems (11). With short sentences, you are not likely to lose track of antecedents when you use pronouns (16). In addition, your reader will not lose track of your point when you write short sentences (16). The flow of thoughts suffers when each sentence is the same length and the same type (16)."

This paragraph is difficult to follow even though each of its sentences, taken one at a time, is clear enough. It fails to hang together. Each sentence seems to be a new beginning, as if none of the sentences had already happened, and the new sentence was starting out in a new direction.

Example:

> "Long, turgid, professorial sentences, that go on endlessly, moving to and around the point and encompassing every viewpoint and several extensive quotations will, if the writer is not careful, try the patience of the reader to the point of exhaustion and rejection, thus losing the objective of inviting the reader to see the point you wish to present in a new and more effective light (65). Writers must focus upon the need to vary their sentences by attending to issues of length and sentence type and to the dangers of multiplying clauses to such an extent that the reader becomes dazed by an overload of information and the sheer flow of words as the writer attempts as best he can to carry the reader to a full understanding of the inter-relatedness of different ideas (68)."

Now, would you like to read the third sentence in this paragraph?

By varying sentences, you keep the reader's mind moving and create a pleasant play of rhythms. Mature writers are expert at varying sentence lengths and types. Think of the voice you are creating as you write; think of the reader's need for drama in your sentences.

A Final Word on Revising

It is all too easy to think of revising as an unpleasant and uncreative chore, like clearing the table after dinner. Writing the essay and grappling with its ideas—that's where the action is. Revising's a bore!

However, once you know what to look for, revising seems more interesting. Catching the little verb doing its insidious work, or finding the verb in disguise, or the sentence twisted into a silly passive form, or the ridiculous misplaced modifier that misdirects meaning. Besides, the difference it will make in your submitted essay is worth all this careful attention.

Few words worth reading or listening to find their way out into the world without the fine craft of revising.

Jefferson may have been inspired, but he also revised. The "Rough Draft" of the Declaration of Independence shows him improving his expression and crystallizing his ideas.

3 The Top Twelve Problems

Introduction

Most handbooks go on for four hundred pages cataloguing every conceivable mechanical and grammatical error and offering explanations for readers already well versed in grammar. The following chapter follows instead the experience of writing teachers who see the same errors in paper after paper, day after day. These twelve errors are our constant companions, so it would be a good idea to get to know them well.

We have kept the explanations simple and offered examples, both of the error and its repair. Since the list is short, students should be able to find what they need easily.

We hope, too, that instructors will become so well acquainted with these pages that they will write "see Problem 7" on a student's paper instead of having to provide an explanation and examples while scribbling in a tight margin and while also having to provide commentary on large order problems.

Problem 1: Spelling

No one would choose to walk around carrying a big sign that said "I am Stupid!" Well, spelling errors do just that for you.

You can have splendid ideas, but if your paper is full of typos and spelling errors, the overall impression will be embarrassing and so will your grade.

Computer Spellcheck both helps and hurts. With Spellcheck, you can catch many errors. But these days teachers feel even less friendly to the occasional typo than they once did.

Use Spellcheck, but remember, it's not perfect.

It will not catch "to" when you intended "too." It's just a dumb machine.

It won't know you thought "them" but typed "then."

Sorry—even in the Age of Technology, you still need to check over your paper.

(Grammarcheck is even worse than spellcheck. Grammarcheck often fusses about correct sentences and leaves you scratching your head trying to figure out what is wrong when nothing is.)

Before the wonders of technology, students had to read their papers out loud. Reading aloud is still a good idea. If you've never done this, you might be amazed at the results. Your ear often catches what your eye misses. However, to read aloud, you need to slow down and read exactly what is on the page instead of reading what you expect to be there.

Read slowly and deliberately.

When you hit a spot that doesn't sound or look right (this method helps also with "grammar" problems), mark it with a pencil. After you've gone through the whole paper, go back and fix what you marked. Avoid fixing mistakes as you go, as that breaks your reading concentration. Plus, when you get to the end, you can go back and see just how many mistakes there are, giving yourself control of the whole task. You might want to start out by reading to a friend or a tutor, but as you improve at this, you can catch errors by reading out loud to yourself.

Another suggestion is to wait until you are revising the essay to focus on spelling and typos. That way, you won't interrupt your flow of thought for minor corrections.

Many bright people are bad spellers, but that doesn't mean they turn in writing loaded with spelling errors. Your readers, rightly or wrongly, will expect you to have used some of these approaches before you submit a paper.

What can you do to help with spelling?

- ✏ keep a list of words you spell poorly (before general dictionaries, people kept their own personal dictionaries of words that caused them trouble—suppose "occasion" and "ocassion" both always look wrong to you!)

✎ check for homonyms (words that sound the same but have different meanings); such as

to—too—two
there—their—they're
affect—effect
accept—except
here—hear
poor—pour—pore

and many more words for common things

✎ recall the rule, "i" before "e" except after "c": so, "piece" but "receive"
✎ use Spellcheck, of course
✎ and always proofread when your mind and eye are alert

Problem 2: Possessives

Do you want to look really bad? Send someone a letter confusing "its" and "it's" or "your" and "you're." For some reason, people who know nothing about grammar will catch these mistakes, and, ridiculous as it may seem, will think you are a dope for making them.

Confusing possessives happens all the time because the rules are not crystal clear. One way to cut down on the amount of "your/you're" and "its/it's" errors you make is to spell out the contraction ("it is" for "it's"; "you are" for "you're"). Most teachers prefer that anyway. Remember, though, that both "your" and "its" show possession.

Examples:

"It's always true that the tiger guards its territory."

"You're going to find that this argument may run counter to your natural inclinations."

49

Other points to remember about possessives:

Case One: For singular noun possessive, the apostrophe goes inside the -s.

Example:

> "The boy's father won eleven dollars in the lottery."
> "John's paper was about Antigone's ethical conflict"

Case Two: The same applies for plural noun possessives that do not end in -s ("people, " "children").

Examples:

> "People's attitudes change as time passes."
> "Children's health care concerns us all."

Case Three: For plural noun possessives ending in -s, the apostrophe goes outside the -s.

Example:

> "The players' contracts expire at the end of the season, and the owners will have to negotiate with each one of them."

Case Four: Remember, inanimate objects can "possess" things. This can be confusing.

Example:

> "The book's main point is relatively simple." This is another way of saying "The main point of the book is relatively simple."

Remember, possessives always translate to "of the ...." So, if you are in doubt, test the meaning of the possessive form ("players", for example) by trying this substitution ("of the players"). Also, if the use of possessive seems awkward (this can happen with inanimate objects), you can always substitute "of the."

Example:

> "They wrote on the document's cover."
>
> Is improved by
>
> "They wrote on the cover of the document."

Warning: Watch out for personal pronouns. Many personal pronouns take possession simply by adding an "s" without an apostrophe ("their/theirs," "her/hers," "who/whose" and, one more time for good measure, "it/its").

Example:

> "After the members of the other party backed down, the candidates knew the election was theirs for the taking."

Case Five: What do we do with joint or multiple possession? The rule allows you to use the possessive form for the last term only.

Example:

> "Siskel and Ebert's recommendations were always valuable."

Problem 3: Subject-Verb Agreement

Usually, making subjects and verbs agree is no problem: either both are singular or both are plural. But things get tougher in sentences like the one you just read. How do you know what the subject is? "Subjects" and "verbs" are both plural, but the subject of the sentence is "making."

Some tricky places to watch for:

Case One: When you have a compound subject that uses "and"– here the verb takes the plural form.

Examples:

> 1   +   1 = plural
> "The conductor and the soloist agree upon the tempo for the Mozart piece."

> "Javelin and long jump are her two best events."

However, some compounds are not plural, when the two or more parts are inseparable:

Examples:

> 1 = singular
> "Rock and roll is here to stay; it will never die."
> "Paper, rock, and scissors is a painful game."

Case Two: When you have a compound subject joined by "or." Here the verb agrees with the latter term.

Example:

> "Either the doctor or his **assistants help** all patients in an emergency."
> "Either the doctor or his **assistant helps** all patients in an emergency."

So remember, if the second term is plural, your verb will be plural. If singular, your verb stays singular.

Case Three: When you have a subject that doesn't look like a normal noun (such as "making"—a noun made from a verb—as in the first sentence in this section), things get tricky.

Example:

> "**Climbing** mountains **takes** courage."

Case Four: When the subject is a pronoun such as "nobody" or "somebody" (also, "anything," "each," "everyone," "much"). In most cases, these pronouns work with a singular verb.

Example:

> "Nobody knows the trouble I've seen."
> "Somebody loves me; I don't know who."
> "Everybody loves my baby."

Case Five: When the subject is a word such as "team" or "jury," which stands for more than one person but functions as singular;

Example:

> "The **jury has** been deliberating all day to reach its verdict."

but

> "The **members** of the jury **have** been deliberating all day to reach their verdict."

Case Six: When the subject follows the verb; for instance, in sentences that start with "There are" or "There is."

Example:

> "There are many factors that influence this argument."

Do yourself and your reader a favor by eliminating the "there are" construction—"Many factors influence this argument."

Case Seven: When many words get in between your subject and verb (an intervening clause).

Example:

> "**The school** that wins the most league games in nine different sports **is** declared conference champion."

For sentences like this, you must take a moment to identify the subject and verb. No easy, quick-fix way of doing this exists, but you can identify these troublesome sentences as you revise your paper.

Warning: Many students have subject-verb agreement problems either because they speak a dialect of English that does not follow these standard rules or they speak languages with different rules. If you find yourself making errors consistently, seek out special assistance. Formal written English does not tolerate subject-verb agreement confusion.

Problem 4: Pronoun Agreement (especially "this," "that," and "it")

Your reader will lose touch if you use pronouns and your reader is not sure what they refer to (the words that pronouns refer to are officially called antecedents, literally "what comes before"). The biggest **problem pronouns** are "this," "that," and "it."

Case One: pronouns must agree with their antecedents.

Example:

> ?   ?
>
> "**The man** at the gate collected all the tickets from the **children. They** then allowed the children to enter the theater."

Revised:

> "The man at the gate collected all the tickets from the children. He then allowed the children to enter the theater."

Case Two: The biggest problem pronouns are "this," "that," and "it."

Example:

> "Kids watch too much television. They play violent video games. They hardly ever eat the right foods. This is the problem in our society."

What does "this" refer to? All three of the things stated before? It is not clear.

Revised:

> "Kids watch too much television. They play violent video games. They hardly ever eat the right foods. All three are problems in our society." or "Parental neglect is the problem in our society"

Warning: Use "this," "that," and "it" carefully, and if you know you have trouble with these three, make an extra effort to check them as you revise (use your computer's "find" function to check).

Case Three: Clarity problems

Sometimes it just isn't clear what you intend.

Example:
    ?   ?

"**Parents** often want their **children** to accomplish **their** dreams." (Whose?)

    ?   ?

"**Anne** told **Carol** that **she** was wrong." (Which one?)

Case Four: Use of he/she (the pronoun gender gap)

One common annoyance for students is how to handle a sentence like this:

"If a student does ___ work, ___ will have success in the class."

If you say "a student does their work," you've messed up (pronoun agreement).

But you don't want to say "his work," because of gender conventions. Do you say "his or her work"? You could, but that becomes annoying after a while.

Solution—turn the antecedent, in this case, the word "student," into a plural:

Revised:

"If **students** do their work, **they** will have success in the class."

Problem 5: Verb Tense Consistency

Verb tense is whether you are writing about the past, present, or future.

- ✐ present: The actors perform a play.
- ✐ past: The actors performed a play.
- ✐ future: The actors will perform a play.

There are also other tense forms to allow you to be more precise about events in time.

Example:

> "The actors will have performed the play by the time she returns."

But most important, keep your tenses the same. Stay consistent in time in your sentences.

Example:

> "They fought the British on the hills and in the depths of the forests. At all times, they keep the enemy guessing about where they will attack next."

This shift from past to present in narration (telling a story) is a common error since either tense is correct.

Revised:

> "They fought the British on the hills and in the depths of the forest. At all times, they kept the enemy guessing about where they would attack next."

Or

> "They fight the British on the hills and in the depths of the forest. At all times, they keep the enemy guessing about where they will attack next."

Make sure that the events/arguments you describe in the paper don't jump around in time. This confuses and distracts your reader.

Problem 6: Sentence Fragments

Your sentences should all be complete statements that can stand on their own. That is easy to say but sometimes tough to do. When you write groups of words that cannot stand on their own and punctuate them as if they were sentences, they are called sentence fragments.

For instance,

Case One: A sentence without a subject:

Examples:

> "Your sentences should all be complete ideas. Easy to say, but sometimes tough to do."

In speech, the group of words "Easy to say, but sometimes tough to do" sounds complete. Writing, however, requires that a group of words marked as a sentence must include a stated (and not merely implied) subject and a definitive verb.

> "The musicians sat up on the stage. Playing their favorite songs to the crowd."

The second group of words belongs to the first group. The easiest solution is to punctuate it differently.

Revised:

> "The musicians sat up on the stage, playing their favorite songs to the crowd."

Case Two: A sentence without a **completing verb.**

Example:

> "The musicians played many wonderful selections. For example, music that was loved equally well by opera lovers and symphony enthusiasts" [constituted the major part of their performance].

These 14 words with a subject ("music") and what appears to be a completing verb ("was loved") ought to qualify as a sentence. However, the material in brackets shows how unfinished the statement is. The word "that" makes everything that follows it part of the subject that needs a completing verb (in this case "constituted").

Trickier fragments are created when a group of words depends on something else.

Case Three: The use of "although" ("because," "since," "while") is one of the biggest problems.

Example:

> "Although the rest of this issue will be decided later," cannot stand on its own.

Revised:

> "We can vote on the main resolutions although the rest of this issue will be decided later."

Spotting fragments can be difficult. They seem correct because in speech they are. Often, the fragment has so many words that somehow it just has to be a full sentence. However, once you spot the fragment, it is easy to repair. Either add the missing element (subject or completing verb), or attach it to the sentence it belongs to.

Warning: you will see fragments in respected prose, fragments used intentionally for emphasis. Advertising is addicted to fragments. In formal prose, however, fragments can confuse your reader. Try to avoid them unless it is obvious to your reader that you are using them for effect.

Problem 7: Comma Splices

Two separate sentences cannot be joined by a weak, little comma. If you do that, the resulting mistake is called a *comma splice*.

Example:

> "They always use violence in films today, they need to develop other ways to capture the attention of the audience."

These two sentences are closely connected and belong together. However, you need something stronger than a comma to indicate how they relate.

Solution One: If the material in the two separate sentences is closely related, join them with a sturdier punctuation mark, the semi-colon.

Revised:

> "They always use violence in films today; they need to develop other ways to capture the attention of the audience."

Warning: Don't overuse the semi-colon. Students discover the semi-colon and then decide that it fits everywhere in their papers, creating a rash of errors.

Solution Two: A simpler fix is to replace the comma with a mighty period.

Revised:

> "They always use violence in films today. They need to develop other ways to capture the attention of the audience."

Solution Three: You can make a higher level correction by adding a conjunction.

Revised:

> "They use violence in films today, but they need to develop other ways to capture the attention of the audience."

Warning: using "however" to join these two sentences creates new problems with punctuation:

Revised:

> "They use so much violence in films today. However, they need to develop other ways to capture the attention of the audience."

or

> "They use so much violence in films today; however, they need to develop other ways to capture the attention of the audience."

By the way, if you don't understand what's so bad about comma splices, listen to someone read aloud a paper that contains several comma splices. The reader will pause awkwardly at the splices, being momentarily confused by the relationship between the ideas. Think of punctuation as road signs that tell the reader (driver) what is coming next (along the road).

Problem 8: Using Conjunctions (also transitions)

Say your friend told you he got an "F" in math. Then he told you he was dropping out of school. You'd probably have some questions. You might ask, "Did failing math cause you to drop out of school?" Or, maybe you'd ask, "Did you know you were dropping out of school, so you gave up on math?" Basically, you'd want to know the connection between those two events.

Your reader wants the same information.

It's one thing to have good ideas, but it's another to show your reader how they relate to each other. That's what conjunctions do.

The basic conjunctions are "and," "but," and "or." These little words can relate entire sentences and powerful ideas. They are like tugboats moving huge ocean liners. Use them wisely.

✏ When the ideas go together (+):

Example:

> "Ships at sea depend upon brave and experienced sailors, and the best technology makes their efforts all the more effective."

✏ When the ideas contrast each other (-):

Example:

> "Ships at sea depend upon the latest technology, but brave and experienced sailors are by far the most important element for success."

✏ When the sentences offer alternatives (x):

60

Example:

> "The success of a ship caught in a mighty storm might depend on technology and experience, or it might depend on the gods that look after the fate of those ready to risk all."

There are a number of other conjunctions you can use to make more precise relationships between sentences, such as

- (-) however, although, nevertheless, on the other hand, in contrast
- (+) moreover, in addition, consequently, in the same way

Sometimes instructors will tell you that your paper lacks **transitions.** Using conjunctions effectively may solve this problem, because what the teacher is saying is that "I don't understand how you move from one idea to the next."

Example:

> "The two nations signed the treaty. The war slowly came to a close. Fighting went on. Several hundred soldiers and civilians died."

This kind of writing becomes tedious and even confusing to your reader because the relationship between ideas is not made clear.

Revised:

> "After the two nations signed the treaty, the war slowly came to a close. But fighting still went on, and several hundred soldiers and civilians died."

> *As you can see, not only did we use the conjunctions "but" and "and," but we also combined the first two sentences by using "after."*

The basic idea is that conjunctions and transitions are part of the "road map" we discussed earlier. You're telling your reader how the ideas in your paper interact with each other.

Problem 9: Quotations

Why do instructors ask you to use sources in your papers? It's to get you used to building up your argument with commentary from experts. Using quotes gives your discussion greater authority. It shows you have done some research and have been thoughtful about the points you are making. But smoothly incorporating quotes into a paper is often a big challenge.

Warning: a quote is used to reinforce a point you want to make in a paper. Don't overdo it with quotes; a good limit is <u>no</u> <u>more</u> <u>than</u> <u>fifteen</u> <u>percent</u> of the total number of words in your paper should be quotation. Don't simply say the same thing twice, once in your own words, once in a quote. Remember, it is your paper and not your quilting together of a patchwork of sources.

Choose quotes wisely. Use a quote when

- ✏ you couldn't say something nearly as well as the quote says it.
- ✏ you want especially to emphasize the point it makes.
- ✏ it proves an unlikely point that your reader might challenge.
- ✏ it proves a point essential to your discussion.

<u>Block</u> <u>quotes:</u> This is a special case, but if you follow this rule it will make your paper much easier to follow. A block quote is set off from your words on the page. You must use it especially for longer quotations (any quote longer than four lines).

Example:

[your words]—The close of the eighteenth century showed the social strains in Britain that come from success and from building a mighty empire. As Brainard and Simpson argue:

A world-wide empire might seem to be what all nations ought to desire. Yet, the 1790s shows a growing strain within English society. As the new rich emerge, gathering fabulous wealth from world trade, the fate of many common people is unpleasant and often tragic. This is no more evident than in the misery of tens of thousands of country people forced to seek their fortune in the commercial cities and the manufacturing towns. (25)

[your words]—The windfall of riches improved the status and living conditions of a few people. However, for many others, this time of change brought great suffering to themselves and to their families.

Block quotes give weight to your paper. Make sure that you introduce them gracefully into your discussion by moving into and away from them smoothly, as in our example.

Incorporated quotes: You must connect the quote to your own sentences. A quote floating by itself—an unanchored quote—loses its context and the reader, and it is bad writing habit.

Examples:

The windfall of riches improved the status and living conditions of a few people. However, for the "tens of thousands of country people forced to seek their fortune in the commercial cities and the manufacturing towns" (25), this time of change brought great suffering to themselves and their families.

or

As Brainard and Simpson have observed, "the 1790s shows a growing strain within English society" (25). While there were many new rich, the plight of the poor spread and deepened to include "tens of thousands of country people" (25).

Warning: Never begin your paragraph with a quotation. This is the worst sort of unanchored quote. Your reader always needs to know how to think about the quoted passage, and how it belongs to the points you are making. The quotations cannot write your paper. You are using them to say what you want to say.

Problem 10: Citing Sources (MLA)

There are several ways to cite sources. Really, the best piece of advice is to find the rules for your particular style, because few people make it a habit of memorizing all of the stylistic conventions of citing. You simply need to know where to look.

A common citing method is MLA (Modern Language Association), which uses in-text citation. Following is a sample with two main styles of MLA **in-text** **citation:**

> "Conventional heroes can be hard to find in late 20th century fiction. This may be because, as Alfred Kazin says, "Many writers see man near the end of the 20th century as a hilariously futile creature, trying by repeated rituals to save himself in a world that majestically ignores him" (246). Some of humanity's frustration may stem from technology, which may be "excluding the human personality in the interest of an idea of Order" (Sypher 231).

As you see, in one case the author's name is in the sentence. In the other, the author's name is in the citation. These in-text citations are used instead of footnotes, and they're kind of handy. The reader immediately knows where you took the information from, because the author's name is right there on the page. If the reader wants to track down the source, the in-text citations refer directly to your works cited page, where you list all sources used in the paper (generally in alphabetical order by author). In-text citation can also be a little easier to use than footnotes when you're typing your paper, as you won't have to do any special formatting.

The works cited page for the material above would look like this:

Works cited

Kazin, Alfred. *Bright Book of Life: American Novelists and Storytellers from Hemingway to Mailer.* Notre Dame, Ind.: University of Notre Dame Press, 1980.
Sypher, Wylie. *Literature and Technology: The Alien Vision.* New York: Random House, 1968.

Make sure you punctuate correctly when you use in-text citations. The important things to remember here are the order of the marks of punctuation: 1) the ending quotation mark; 2) the citation, in parenthesis: either just the page number (no "p." is needed) or author's name, space (no comma), page number; and 3) the sentence's ending punctuation mark (usually a period). Again, it looks like this: "... ending word" (Smith 16).

There are many other rules for MLA, and, again, we suggest you review a list of MLA rules if you are doing extensive citing.

Problem 11: Locating Your Thesis (Hint: in your first draft, it's probably at the end)

You probably have struggled to define your thesis clearly at one time or another (or maybe this happens all the time). Don't think for one minute that you are alone. Often, a person starts writing (whether it's an angry letter to the editor, a column for a newspaper, or an essay for class) with just a kernel of an idea. OK, you say, well then how do they make that idea clear?

The answer: They write.

Writing and learning are linked at the hip. Some even argue that you never learn about something as well as when you are writing about it. Think about this next time you are staring at a blank computer screen or piece of paper. To get to something good to say (see part 1), you have to write.

A 100% natural consequence of this is that your best ideas often come near the end of things: the main point is at the end of a sentence; a topic sentence is at the end of a paragraph; and, most commonly, your thesis is at the end of the first draft of your essay.

This, again, is 100% natural and useful. The only way this tendency can work against you is if you let it—or if you don't start writing.

As you tackle a paper, start to write (see part 1). If you are shaky about your main idea, don't worry. Don't be surprised if that main idea shows up in the very last paragraph of the first draft you write—and once you feel confident, you may even come to expect to find it there.

Problem 12: Paragraph Development

Each paragraph in your essay should have a defined function, and readers expect that paragraphs are like little essays. Teachers will complain that a paragraph lacks unity. By this they mean that the paragraph wanders off or does not have a topic or purpose of its own.

Your paragraphs should signal to your reader what the different parts of your discussion are. One good test is to try to form a topic outline (or a reverse outline) after you have written your paper. If you cannot tell where one or more of your paragraphs fit, or even what they are doing, then you have revision work to do.

The paragraphs in your essay should be clear and focused. There are many ways to address this issue (and thus many ways to fall into this problem), but make sure that your paragraphs have good topic sentences, or that the main idea of each paragraph is clearly stated. While there are solid reasons to vary the placement of your topic sentences—sometimes in the beginning, middle, or end of a paragraph—most topic sentences will be at the beginning of a paragraph.

Example: Thesis paragraph of the paper:

> "Many city parking authorities are examples of how government can exploit people. City governments should not make parking a way of generating revenue from its citizens, but they do by stacking the deck through unreasonable parking rules and time limits, aggressive ticket writers, a complex bureaucracy that makes a "not guilty" plea difficult, allowing only a few days to make payment (often less than a week), and high penalties for late tickets. While parking must be enforced in cities, aggressive parking authorities create many victimless offenses. Government should be focused on protecting law-abiding citizens, but by making parking tickets a business, governments are exploiting these very citizens."

Sample paragraph in this essay:

> "The city can be a tough place to find a place to park, and a strict parking system makes people not want to visit the city. Parking authorities prey on law-abiding citizens, essentially billing them for minor offenses. Parking authorities target

those they know will pay: those who have registered cars and who do not want to run afoul of the law. These authorities create a city parking system of unreasonably short meter times and complicated rules about when parking is restricted. These rules are deliberately complex, as the parking authorities are trying to lure law-abiding visitors to park so as to generate revenue from them."

What commonly happens is that you know what you are talking about, but the start of the paragraph doesn't show this. Based on the example above, the writer seems to say that the paragraph is going to be about the challenge of finding a place to park when going to the city. By the end, the paragraph is really about how authorities create complex parking rules to trip-up and exploit law-abiding citizens. But the reader will be confused because what appears to be the topic sentence—or the road sign indicating what the paragraph is about—is misleading.

As you review your paper, look at each paragraph. Identify the topic sentence, and ask yourself a few questions:

- ✎ Is this sentence, in fact, what the paragraph is about?
- ✎ Does this sentence help you to prove what you are trying to accomplish in the essay?

You can think of the structure of your essay as following the argument outlined in your topic sentences. Remember what you are trying to prove in the paper: that's what each of your topic sentences should reflect.

Warning: you may have problems with topic sentences if you tend to write a lot of skimpy paragraphs. A paragraph should say something, and if you can't devote more than a sentence or two, you probably need to expand upon your thought, creating a more comprehensive topic sentence.

This completes our Twelve Top Problems. There are many more we could have mentioned. However, at some point, the more you mention the more confusing it all becomes. These twelve appear most often and have the most serious impact on student papers. Gaining control of these problems represents a major accomplishment in your development as a writer.

4 The Secrets of "A" Students

Introduction

The following section of <u>The</u> <u>Writing</u> <u>Tutor</u> may be more valuable to you than what you have read so far. In this section you will learn important truths about being a successful student and maximizing the results of your hard work.

Some students seem to know these strategies for success, either because previous schooling has emphasized them or because their upbringing has made these outlooks obvious. Too many students, however, with talent and promise, fail to show themselves to advantage in school. So called "late bloomers"—that is, students who suddenly begin to excel after years of weak performance—are usually students who come upon these important lessons and only then begin to shine.

This section intends to welcome you into the secrets that highly successful students know. The advice here will be more useful than the usual encouragement to "try harder" or to "apply yourself" to your work or even to begin to "take yourself seriously" although all that is excellent advice. Instead, we intend to suggest specific things you can do to upgrade your work and achieve better grades.

Time Management

You can take all the fine advice this book lays out for you, but if you fail to use your time properly nothing much will come of it.

Not so long ago, most students spent all their time being students. Now, almost all students work—sometimes full-time jobs—in addition to being full-time students. Students have families of their own, or responsibilities for parents or grandparents. Some travel long distances to school. So, disciplined time management is essential.

Nothing emphasizes time issues as forcefully as writing assignments. The difference between you and the dummy sitting next to you who somehow earns higher grades may be nothing more than time management.

Professional writers give themselves time for first drafts, and multiple drafts after that, not to mention editing and proofreading. Students, with nothing like the skills and experience of professionals, start working the night before the assignment is due. The results for students are predictable—half-baked concepts, disorderly presentation, and baggy prose, littered with errors.

Teachers usually assign papers al least a week before the due date and assume that students will begin work on the paper right away. You would be wise to use that week strategically.

Papers need time to brew. You cannot start too early to think about the paper and begin to make notes. A half-hour of thinking and jotting down thoughts on the first night of the assignment week starts you off. You will find your mind working on the ideas and churning away at sentences while you fold the laundry, wash the car, check out groceries. This quiet, subconscious labor will take you far into the project before you know it.

You need to attempt a draft several days before the due date. If it helps, make believe this is informal writing and not a draft (See Part I). You might want to work at different parts of the paper in no particular order. Again, a half-hour here and there will do.

A formal first draft, however, is due (for you, not for the teacher) at least two days before submission. Write it out, and put it away. Use the next day for focusing on

- the order of the materials,
- source material,
- challenges to your thesis and answers to those challenges,
- building strong opening paragraphs, and
- the conclusion.

Now you are ready for the night before due date. This is the time for serious revision. Check the decisions you made the previous night, and finally, polish those sentences to a fine glow. It is probably a good idea to write past the word limit on your previous draft. You should find that in the final draft you will be cutting words as you clear out repetition and uncertain constructions (See Part II). You may be adding substance, but you will certainly be cutting words.

Finally, leave time to proofread. Remember, Spellcheck cannot really do this for you, and you need to be alert for this mechanical task. If you are tired, what is on the page, errors and all, will look good to you. If you find your mind wandering and your eyes blurring (or shutting), pack it in and save the last proofread for next morning. Of course, that probably means setting the alarm for a half-hour earlier.

Students know they should use a sensible process to produce their best work, but too often fail to use their time efficiently. Teachers have become accustomed to miserable, sloppy work submitted as final copy, but they save the good grades for papers done with care.

The Secrets of Writing "A" Exams

An important part of your success in school depends on taking exams well. So many students seem to know the material well and to participate well in class discussion and group work only to have the misfortune of writing poor exams. Teachers talk often about this gap. The following discussion about preparing for and writing exams intends to do something about this problem.

Preparing for an Exam

Do you find yourself wondering, "what's going to be on the exam?" The answer is usually right in front of you. Just ask yourself:

- ✏ What has the teacher been talking about?
- ✏ What is in your notes?
- ✏ What questions were raised in class?
- ✏ Which were settled, and how?

In most courses, these simple questions will tell you what's on the exam.

The question—"what's going to be on the exam?"—comes from a sense of panic rather than from logic. While the teacher could ask you anything, including materials from the reading that he never mentioned, almost always, what has gone on in class will appear again on the exam.

1. Gathering Information

There are instances where material in the reading that was not discussed will appear. In these cases the undiscussed material is likely to be important to the presentation in the textbook. While some teachers will try to fool you by asking you about obscure matters, this is rare. Nevertheless, you might want to quiet your fears by asking the teacher whether you are responsible, first, for materials that were not discussed in class; and, second, for "minor points such as ....or more major issues such as ...." You may as well go ahead and ask. If you ask the question in this way and provide good examples of major and minor points, you will impress your teacher.

Teachers hate it when students ask continually "will this be on the exam?" Nevertheless, there are several questions you can ask that will help you determine what your teacher wants you to do. Teachers routinely assume that you already know what the exam will look like, even when they themselves haven't even constructed the exam.

Some obvious questions include:

- ✏ Will this be an open book exam?
- ✏ Will we be permitted to use our notes?
- ✏ Does the exam cover all the material or only what we have covered since the last exam?
- ✏ Will the exam be restricted to material we have covered in class?
- ✏ Will it include such things as....?

You might want to parcel out these questions among several classmates rather than ask them all yourself. You may be surprised to find a happy reception to these questions from your teacher. And the questions help the teacher, often, to decide what exactly he or she is going to test and how.

2. Studying Effectively

Once you have settled in your mind what will surely be on the exam, what is likely, and what is possible, you can begin loading up for the essay you can foresee writing

It may be a good idea to study together with others in the class. However, be sure you choose someone who has impressed you as knowledgeable and interested in the course material. Studying with losers will help you lose. Most teachers will be delighted that several students bother to gather to review the class she has been teaching. This is not cheating in any way. If the material is particularly dense and difficult, you might want to ask whether the teacher will answer questions that emerge from group study (e-mailing questions to the teacher helps). In some cases, teachers are happy to arrange a study session for groups of students who want to meet with the teacher to review materials before the exam. Teachers respond favorably to requests for assistance that focuses on the material. Teachers admire students who demonstrate a special effort to learn.

What sorts of things will impress the exam reader? First off, be sure you know the correct name for things, concepts, or people and how to spell these names. Just go through the text and your notes and make a list of all names. If there are processes in your material, be sure to review the order of the process (the narrative). And finally, pick out several quotes and do your best to memorize them. A quotation dropped into an exam essay, even though not precisely accurate, will make your teacher sit up and take notice.

Writing Exams

Teachers hate it when students finish early, write little, and leave. Many students believe, apparently, that getting to the bottom line quickly is the best way to write an exam. Or, maybe, they just want to escape from the room. In either case, writing little and leaving early is a recipe for disaster.

The best approach is to **Show What You Know (SWYK)**. Every exam essay is really asking you to do two things:

- ✒ First, to answer the question, and
- ✒ Second, to show your familiarity with the material.

This second goal is often unexpressed by the exam question since teachers take it for granted that you will use the exam to show off and impress the teacher with what you know.

Suppose you are asked to write on the following topic:

> The Ten Commandments are in reality about several different kinds of transgressions. Classify the commandments into their separate concerns, and explain the logic of their ordering. Be sure to refer to specific commandments in your essay.

Incomplete essay #1 (answers the question but without specifics)

"The Ten Commandments are about several different kinds of transgressions. Some pertain to the nature of God and how to praise him and show our devotion. One focuses upon family obligations. Others concern our behavior towards one another. And, finally, there are two that address our internal dispositions and not our acts.

The first several talk about God and our devotions because without a commitment to God none of the remaining commandments makes sense. Family, too, is important and requires devotion and loyalty. Behavior towards others is another way to show, in everyday actions, how obedient we are. And, finally, our ability to control our internal desires proves our complete obedience to God and his laws.

While many people know the Ten Commandments, it is also important to think about how to classify them and what these sequence of commandments means. Once we discover the central theme—the complete obedience to God and His laws—we can understand much better the good sense contained in them."

Comment: This essay answers the question very well. Nevertheless, the writer has not bothered to show what she knows in detail. The answer is conceptually complete but does not prove close knowledge of the Ten Commandments and how they work. A grader might even assume that the essay represents a playback of class notes with no real understanding.

Incomplete Essays #2 (detail without answering the question)

"When Moses arrives at Mt. Sinai, the Israelites are in terrible shape. They have shown evidence of every sort of transgression. They fight among themselves, steal, lie, show cowardice, and most of all show their disobedience. How many times has God proven His devotion to them? He parts the Red Sea and drowns their enemies. He causes manna to fall from the sky to feed them in the desert wilderness. He brings forth water from a rock. And still, the Israelites complain about their liberation. He even promises them that he will make them into His "Chosen People" and "on wings of eagles" he will deliver them.

Indeed, God's greatest gift to them is the law of the Ten Commandments. Here God instructs His people, and all people ever after who would follow Him, on the Laws of Life. This is the very essence of the Torah, which means "Guide to Life."

What are these lessons? The people must have no other Gods before Him; they must pray to Him on a special day called the Sabbath; they are not to use His name casually or to curse another or to tell lies, swearing in God's name. Also, the people are to honor their parents. They should not murder or steal or commit adultery or lie in court in testimony against their neighbor. And, finally, the people should not harbor desires—covet—for their neighbors' goods or their wives.

God promises that if the Israelites will obey all these laws, He will make them a great nation. Given how difficult these laws are for us to follow, if the people can obey them, they will already be a great nation."

Comment: This essay shows an impressive amount of detail of the story and of the Ten Commandments. However, if you look closely, you will see that the student failed to answer the question. The student neither classified the commandments nor explained what this classification teaches us.

Exam Strategies

Be sure to observe the time boundaries for the exam. Teachers will often designate either time limits or point values to each question or part of the exam. Students who do poorly often fail because they stay on one part of the exam too long and never get to the rest. If one essay is worth 20 percent, give it 20 percent of the time available for the exam.

As with writing assignments generally, be sure you understand exactly what the question wants you to do. Look for the **command words** (See Part I). Observe carefully what is not mentioned as well as what is. Exam questions tend to be far more precise in their boundaries than essay questions done at home. **Don't wander**; focus.

Occasionally, the exam topic is not clearly expressed. It is fair for you to ask questions before you start writing to clarify the exam question. Don't, however, say, "I don't understand what you want!" Focus on what specifically is puzzling you. It helps to ask, "when you write ... in the question, do you mean us to discuss ...?" Be precise; it shows you know things and have an interest in doing well.

Take a few moments to map out your answer. Although you don't have time for an elaborate outline, you can at least list the items you must include to answer the question and to show your knowledge effectively. Think of it as a checklist rather than an outline.

Taking a few moments to map your essay will allow you to write more, and more effectively than if you dive right in. Students often feel they should not waste a moment but start writing immediately. Often these students write less than others who take a few moments to plan.

Try your best to reserve time at the end to review what you have written. Writing in haste and under pressure can deform your prose badly. Thoughts come so much faster than the sentences that hold them. Look for mechanical errors, but look too for sentences with words or whole phrases omitted. Often you will have written words you did not intend, so find some time to fix them. Such after-care will impress your teacher.

A Note on Handwriting

Students assume that content is everything. Imagine, however, your teacher reading these exams, perhaps fifty or a hundred of them, late at night when the scribblings in exam booklets begin to crawl around on the page like ants and spiders. Test essays that are written clearly and with space left in margins and between sections of the exam will often score better than they deserve simply because they appear more readable.

Another way to think of this is to be considerate of the teacher. Reading exams is far more difficult and unpleasant than writing them. Anything that makes your teacher's task easier has to help.

If you want to shine, take exams seriously. Your teacher does.

The Secret Rules, or What Teachers Look for

In most games the players know the basic rules, but there are secret rules that only the best players know. In Atlantic City casinos, the proprietors are careful to identify those players who understand the secrets of "blackjack" well enough to beat the casino regularly. These players are banned. The casinos are happy enough to have players who know the basic rules but do not understand the game.

This distinction between those who know enough to play and those who know enough to win carries through most activities in life, and being a student certainly is one of them. Teachers generally know the rules and what it takes to win. Also, teachers, unlike casino operators, want you to win and wouldn't mind having to give every student an "A". However, teachers themselves may never have made clear to themselves, let alone their students, what these secret rules are.

The cloudiness about these insider's rules makes being a student a hard game to play. Suppose that for once a teacher who knew the secret rules would tell you just what you had to do to win. Would you pay attention? Well, please do; that is exactly what is about to happen.

Secret #1 Never do school work as if it were school work.

Like most secret rules, this maneuver is far from obvious and seems peculiar. After all, you are a student in a classroom, and everything about school is, as they say, "academic." The classroom is removed from "the real world"; but what happens in the classroom can have as deep an impact as anything in life.

The student who plays the classroom game as if it were only a game is already in trouble. Work as if what you are doing is the ultimate reality. For example, ask questions that really are questions. The worst classroom question in all the world is "will this material be on the exam?"—or its variant, "will we be responsible for this material?" You might as well say: "I have no interest, Mr. Teacher, in what you are teaching; I am here only for the grade and because my curriculum requires it." Follow the path of your curiosity and find the real questions that sit within the material. Stay alert and engaged.

The same holds true for the papers you write. There is a species of writing called "the school essay" that all instructors know well. According to the rules never spoken, this essay receives a "C+", even if it has few errors, simply because nothing real happens in it.

Teachers recognize the "school essay" from several identifying marks that almost always appear together. They are the following:

Mark 1. The writer is uninvolved

Example:

> "There are three ways in which religious instruction can be beneficial to a person. In the following paper, I will analyze these three ways and show how they can help a person lead a better life. In my conclusion, the reader will see why he or she can benefit from observing these three reason why following religious instruction is a good idea."
>
> **The first reason why religious instruction can be beneficial....**
>
> **The second reason ....**
>
> **And lastly, the third reason.....**
>
> **In conclusion, the three reasons ....."**

You have just met the famous **Five Paragraph Monster.** This kind of essay fails to satisfy, not because it is disorderly or incorrect but because it is painfully dull and unreal. The writer has no interest in the topic; he is going through the motions, writing a "school paper." He has done his very least, but worst of all, he has said to the teacher: "I have no interest in what you teach and who you are" to a person whose life's commitment is to interest students in materials they at first knew and cared nothing about. You can't imagine how heart-breaking it is for teachers to read essays that show no interest. How could the teacher applaud you in return?

A course paper is not a horizontal spelling test, where you will do well if you avoid mechanical errors. Your writing must show real interest and engagement.

Mark 2: The writer is too involved

In this case the writer fails to establish distance; as a result, the reader cannot relate to or be persuaded by a view that seems so limit-ed to the writer. The writer assumes a stance of values but only for the purpose of producing a school paper.

Example:

> "As a person who has had to struggle all her life just to get by, I think it is outrageous how some people who do well in the world just don't care about others. Just because they had it easy doesn't mean that other people don't deserve consid-eration and respect. Just the other day, a well dressed woman looked at me with a sour look on her face because my clothes were not expensive and fancy enough for her. If we are ever to have justice in America, all people need to be treated the same."

Now we have engagement, but it is empty and thoughtless and inap-propriate as a piece of writing for school.

But how do you manufacture interest when it isn't there in the first place?

Secret #2. "Real World" Connections

Effective teachers connect the course material to significant issues in the world and in the lives of students. Occasionally students mistake these efforts to find connections for filler or comic relief. Teachers who dramatize the concepts they teach find too often that their students remember the story but miss the concept the story illustrates. While there are teachers who live so completely in the abstract that they provide few examples, good teachers do both.

Whether your teacher has provided "real world" connections or not, your job is to recognize them. Otherwise, your studies will never become real to you, and the work you do will appear merely formal to others.

You have to ask as you read, as class discussion goes on, as you plan your paper

- what does this topic have to do with me and the people around me?
- what differences would it make if this issue went one way or the other?
- who cares about this, and why?

You may discover, too, that academic matters are closer to the life around you than you think. If you haven't explored these basic questions, your paper is likely to appear a mere exercise and bore you, your teacher, and any imaginable reader to tears.

Secret #3. Secrets of Academic Culture

Academic culture, you may have noticed, differs in important ways from everyday life. Fail to notice the difference and you won't succeed in school and in your writing. What are the main features of academic culture?:

- Academics don't rush to conclusions; instead, they delay conclusions for as long as possible in order to explore fully all issues and all sides to all related questions. This may look like a silly game, but its purpose is serious. This refusal to jump to conclusions is fundamental to the search for truth. Jumping

to conclusions will land you in a ditch. Always
ask: "How else might I look at this question?"

☞ Academics look at matters from all possible perspectives,
especially from all the perspectives of those involved in
what they are studying. Always ask: "How would others
look at this?"

☞ Academics resist common wisdom, for which they have
earned a reputation for "ivory tower" arrogance.
Academics think that whatever is commonly believed
must be wrong. They love to challenge generally
accepted ideas in order to extend knowledge
beyond conventional understanding. Always ask: "What
can I discover about this that others commonly miss?"
Think "while most people believe X, careful examination
reveals Y to be true."

☞ Academics see the search for new ideas as an adventure,
as thrilling and uncharted as anything in "Indiana
Jones." Always ask: "where is the drama, where is the
adventure, in this paper I am writing?"

While these four features don't exhaust the portrait of academic
culture, they provide you clear guides to joining this odd but noble
community. Not only will adopting the customs of academic culture
help you as a student, it will provide you powers for success elsewhere.

Secret #4. The Secret of Who You Are

This question—"Who Are You?"—from the caterpillar in <u>Alice in
Wonderland</u> is essential for most students looking to succeed in college. Many students defeat themselves before the race is even run by
assuming that their own background disqualifies them from writing
well and succeeding in higher education. Too many think: "I don't belong
here; college is for other folks!"

One of the wonders of our present moment in education in the
United States is that no one has to feel this way, and most teachers
are happy to welcome all voices into the academic choir. Almost all
teachers, even the ones who seem snobbish—usually because they use
precise language and know a great deal—are happy with the energies
and fundamental questions that newcomers to their academic world
bring to the discussion.

If, in class discussion or in thinking through the writing assignment, you come upon an experience that is true to you but as yet unimagined by the book or the teacher, you have a wonderful opportunity to teach the learned something. Over the years, learning has been fed from below more often and more vitally than from libraries full of books. It may help to think that adding your voice and your experience to the discussion is not only a strategy for success but a responsibility you have as a student. Your teacher will be delighted with your effort when it is honest and thoughtful. Be real.

Secret #5. What Have You Read and Thought About?

Teachers love what they call **"inter-textual" agility** in a discussion or in a student paper. If you can bring one writer to focus upon another and make both of them useful to the point you want to make, your teacher will be very pleased. This shows you have made your reading useful to you and to the discussion you are having with your reader. This act of widening the discussion is the loveliest part of academic culture. So, use your sources and use them well—which means, use them as if they were people thinking, just like you and your reader.

Example:

> In The Communist Manifesto, Karl Marx objects angrily to the way workers are turned into mere "appendages of the machine." In the process, human beings lose their most precious characteristic, their capacity for creative labor, and become instead mere robots. Adam Smith, in The Wealth of Nations (1776), thought it was just wonderful that work had been specialized and that each worker now carried out a petty and meaningless task in producing thousands of thumb tacks, all day long, year after year. Marx, in contrast, already sees the little worker portrayed by Charlie Chaplin in the film, Modern Times (1936). He sees the worker, wrenches in hands, spasmodically twitching through his lunch break as if he himself has become a machine. He sees poor Charlie snaking his way through the gears of the machine that has become his master.

Secret #6 When an "A" is not an "A"

With grade inflation, "A's" mean less than they used to. Alert students set their goal higher. But what is higher than an "A"? The answer is an enthusiastic recommendation from your instructor. To move on to graduate or professional school or to a choice employment opportunity, you will need letters of recommendation. The best letters come from teachers who know who you are, who admire your personal character, and who can praise your work in specific terms. So, make yourself known to your instructors, and save copies of your best work so your teacher's recommendation letter can include details. Most of all, don't be shy about your talents. Teachers feel honored when asked by their best students to write such letters.

Summing Up

These secrets have more to do with understanding who you are and who your teachers are than with any special writing or studying technique. They have to do with claiming ownership of learning and the institutions of your schooling. While we have tried our best to recommend some particular strategies while exploring their secrets, the essential ingredient to all of them is your willingness to see yourself as a person who has as much right as anyone to shine. The essential ingredients are courage and imagination.

Appendix

Essay #1

The following essay is an example of a **one-sided** **argument**. Note also how the use of certainty words raises doubts rather than provide a sense of assurance. Finally, the tone is far too chatty to sustain a trustworthy argument.

At the same time, this essay does some things well. What strengths can you find in this essay?

Assignment:

In the modern university, some have argued, students are customers and need to be treated with that in mind. Others, however, have argued that thinking of students as customers is having a bad effect on higher education. Adopt a position in this debate and attempt to convince your reader that the position you have taken is the correct one.

> I strongly believe that the reality is that students are customers and deserve to be treated with the care and respect that the customers of any business deserve. After all, students pay large tuition bills, and just this fact alone entitles them to say whether the product and services they are purchasing are the correct ones. If you go into a store to purchase something, don't you have the right to buy it or not, depending on whether it pleases you? Therefore, it ought to be clear to anyone that the customer is always right and that in this case the student who is the customer has the ability to decide what the educational product is and whether the service that delivers it [the teacher and the course] is satisfactory.
>
> It may once have been true that the student had to obey simply any of the rules and accept whatever the school and teachers did. In college, however, all that changes. In high school students don't pay for their education, and besides they aren't old enough to decide what they should learn and how. Nevertheless, in college, students do pay huge tuition bills and in many cases large sums for housing and fees and supplies. Recent figures show that many elite Universities and colleges charge nearly $25,000 a year just for tuition. State

Universities, once almost free, now charge up to $7,000 a year for tuition. This gives students the right to say what their education should be. It's like the golden rule. Whoever has the gold rules! And if students don't like what they are getting, they can always go to another school that can deliver the goods.

Besides, a lot of people don't realize that students in college are old enough to make up their own minds about what to study and how they should be taught. Nowadays many college students are quite grown up and some are actually adults returning to school after they have worked and started a family. It is absurd to think that adults need to be told what to do and what they should want.

Also, in today's world students know much more about things than in previous times. We grow up faster than any generation in earlier days. We know a lot about politics and sex and violence that people in older times didn't want to experience or even think about. Educators sometimes forget how advanced students are in their thinking. Why should we be treated as if we are children?

Customers in all situations control their purchases. Even when they are spending not much money, the customer should be made to feel that he or she is the boss and be catered to by the person who owns the business. That is how free enterprise works in America. If you go into a restaurant, you should be able to expect good food and friendly service. Even if the waiter is having a bad day personally, he must be pleasant and helpful and smiling. In the same way, the customer gets to pick what he wants from the menu. To have the waiter tell him what he wants to eat would certainly be absurd and the customer would have a perfect right to be offended and walk out.

In the same way, students as customers, have the right to determine which courses to take. In addition, within those courses, they have a right to determine how much and what kind of work they should be asked to do. The teacher should learn to listen to the students about how to use class time.

86

Some professors like to lecture and many students find that boring. If the students learn better by having a discussion or by group activities, they should request that kind of class from the professor. If the work is too hard, or if the grades cause the students too much anxiety, the professor should listen to his customers and scale back the work and grade more leniently. Finally, the teacher should listen to the students about what is important in the material. It is the instructor's job to please the student as much as possible. After all, who is paying the bill?

It is clear, then, that the person who pays has the right to say what he is paying for. So, in education, as in everything else, the customer is king.

Essay #2

This second essay develops a **more balanced arguement.** Why is this a better paper? How many different things does this writer do well?

Are there any ways to improve this essay?

Assignment:

In the modern university, some have argued, students are customers and need to be treated with that in mind. Others, however, have argued that thinking of students as customers is having a bad effect on higher education. Adopt a position in this debate and attempt to convince your reader that the position you have taken is the correct one.

Students pay higher tuition today in order to attend college than ever before. They spend months looking carefully through catalogues, shopping for the school of their choice. When they decide which school to "buy", they certainly would seem to have the customer's right to be treated with consideration by the institution and by their professors. However, at that point the comparison of students with customers begins to fall apart because of the nature of what students have purchased. In the deeper sense, students cannot be considered to be customers.

Students and their families invest $25,000 in tuition alone for the privilege of attending America's elite colleges and universities, and even the public universities can cost $7,000 annually. At these prices, the purchaser shares rights and expectations common to customers in all other areas. They should receive what they have bargained for and what has been advertised by the seller of these services. They should be treated in a courteous and helpful manner, and their needs should be attended to. If they are dissatisfied, they have a right, as has any customer, to complain and to receive satisfaction.

However, the comparison with customers of other kinds of products and services begins to break down when we consider what college tuition has purchased. Does the tuition payment entitle the student to determine the content of courses, the curricular requirements, the standards that are applied to evaluating student work, or the teaching approach of the professor? In order to settle this question, we might first investigate other cases where paying the bill does not carry with it the requirement to be made happy.

When we pay our taxes we purchase, among other things, police protection. It is surely the case that we pay the salaries of the policemen who patrol our highways. Now suppose you are stopped for a traffic violation. Would it make much sense to object to the officer that he should not write you a ticket because you pay his salary? Besides the practical fact that the officer would find your argument absurd, it is also the case that your argument is untrue. Your tax payment did not purchase a freedom from being ticketed for breaking the law. Instead, it purchased the patrolling of the highways to protect you and everyone else from those who would break the law. In this case, you have broken the law, and so, unpleasant as it might seem, you have paid the officer's salary to ticket you.

When you go to the dentist's office, you often have an unpleasant experience. It would not make sense, however, to tell the dentist not to drill because you are paying for his services. His job is not to make you comfortable and happy but to care for your teeth. And this might include all sorts of painful procedures. What you have purchased is the dentist's expert ability to make you healthy.

These two instances can help us think about whether the college student is a customer and where that analogy fails. Although college students would treasure the freedom to choose their courses and resist all course requirements, the curriculum has been designed by experts who know what courses students need and how one course leads to another. In the same way, while students would like to decide how much work and how well done is sufficient for successful grades, it is the professor who knows enough to set these standards and make the appropriate judgments. Like the dentist, the professor can be presumed to know the technique of his craft. After years of experience and some training, the instructor knows when free discussion is appropriate and when lecture is the answer. Students might even fail or receive low grades. Here the professor acts like the police officer, "ticketing" those who are not performing well so that those who are can get ahead. Credentials, to mean anything, need to be reserved for those who earn them.

Are students customers? Yes, and no. Most of all, students need to understand what being a student means and what they have "purchased." The college experience should be pleasant and enriching, but it can be so only when the faculty can make available their best talents to students, and sometimes that is neither comfortable or painless. However, that is what the tuition payment has purchased in the first place.

Essay #3

The following paper suffers from many of the errors we have covered in Part II (Revision) and Part III (Twelve Top Errors) of this book.

If you were revising, repairing errors, and proofreading, what would you fix?

Don't be surprised if the first time through you don't see much wrong; by the time you have had a good look you will see several dozen atrocities. If you see all the problems all at once, you should immediately apply for a job grading papers.

Assignment:

Many people today are skeptical about how revolutionary the American revolution really was. After all, the revolution was made by men of substance and failed to address the rights of women, of the poor, and of enslaved African people in the colonies. Review Jefferson's <u>Declaration of Independence</u> in order to understand what revolutionary claims it is making for its own time and for ours.

It is well known to pretty much everyone that the <u>Declaration of Independence</u> was written by Thomas Jefferson in 1776. In the document, it was stated that the people are in possession of rights which are in existence in order to make them free. It was thought by some people at that time that only the King was able to claim to have rights. Nevertheless, it was Thomas Jefferson who stated that it was the people themselves who were able to reach decisions about the issues that especially concerned them.

Right from the opening of the <u>Declaration of Independence</u> we can see that Jefferson was trying to state that there are rights that exist for the people and are supported by "the Laws of Nature and of Nature's God." Furthermore, Jefferson says that the rights he is talking about are so clear to people that they are "self-evident." Moreover, clear to anyone who looked into the matter.

In what follows, he then goes on to state what these rights are. To quote from the document: "We hold these truths to be self-evident, that all men are created equal, that they are endowed by their Creator with certain unalienable rights, that among these are life, liberty and the pursuit of happiness. That to secure these rights, governments are instituted among men, deriving their powers from the consent of the governed."

This is the very thing that makes the document that Jefferson put down in writing so very revolutionary. Because without these writes there wouldn't be any freedom for us in the first place. Besides, if "all men are created equal" as Jefferson states, then no one is any different from anyone else in respect to what rights they get to have.

We should take note that when the rights are listed by Jefferson they can be put together into three basic categories: life, liberty, and the pursuit of happiness. Listing them this way is revolutionary. The right to life means that everyone should be allowed to live and that no one can take your life, especially the government. It is trying to say that your life is precious to you and that is very important. The second right which Jefferson mentions in the <u>Declaration of Independence</u> has to do with liberty. When he is mentioning liberty Jefferson states that everyone is allowed to do whatever he wants, unless you want to yell fire in a building that is not burning. Otherwise, he is free not to have to do what someone else wants him to do. And finally, the pursuit of happiness. With this right you can choose to do things according to what you think is right, even when what has been chosen by you might be wrong to somebody else. So, you can now see that these rights are truly revolutionary.

I will now show some of the other rights that make this declaration which was written by Jefferson so very very revolutionary. He says next that just in case their is the possibility that the government does go bad, you can fix it. Jefferson states: "That whenever any form of government becomes destructive of these ends, it is the right of the people to altar or abolish it." When he goes so far as to be saying that the people can have a revolution if they would like to do so, then the people are in possession of the right to make happen whatever form of government that seems to be the best for themselves. It is saying that the people can make a decision about anything at all that pleases them to exist at that time.

Further along in the document Jefferson wrote, he states that if a government seems wrong to them, then they can do the following: "But when a long train of abuses and usurpations, evinces a design to reduce them under absolute despotism, it is their right, it is their duty, to throw off such government." Anyone who thought about this would clearly agree that this is a revolutionary thing to be saying. The people would be in the position of having the right to rule. A revolution, for sure.

It is true that some kinds of people were not singled out for having rights. If Jefferson was writing his declaration today, he would be sure to mention women, minorities, and gay people. He would have to do that because if he were to leave anybody out than they would not be in possession of all the rights that belong to all the people. It is important to understand that if anybody was left out it could no longer be true that "all men are created equal." And it would be an incomplete revolution.

Nobody should ever think of doubting that the American Revolution was really a revolution. We are told by Jefferson that we have rights from God, next he states for the reader what those rights are, and then he tells us that if these rights are in the process of being taking away we can rebel and make a revolutionary change in things for our own betterment and to get for us the rights which were given to us originally by God.

Essay #4

This sample is the opening of an essay recently submitted by a bright student who did not have the benefit of reading this book. What has gone wrong? How can you tell this is an **early draft** and never should have been submitted?

Please go ahead and write in your revisions in the spaces provided. Go ahead and be the teacher.

Adam Smith and the Free Economy

In everyday life people have to deal with the capitalistic

system of the economy. The basic free market system is how

people buy, sell and trade goods and services. Adam Smith

wrote a lot about a market economy, but his idea of the way

a totally free market should work was not necessarily the way a totally "free" market works in today's world. Smith's main problem with the way that the economy works today would be that it is not really a true free market. Two of the main things that Smith deals with in his writing is that of monopolies and tariffs. Adam Smith contends that these two problems hinder the way a market is supposed to naturally work.

Both monopolies and tariffs come about because of government interference in the market. Governments of countries set tariffs to help out the domestic producers of products. This then brings about a monopolistic control over where the goods are coming from. Smith does say that this can helps certain companies in the short run, but does not produce the best overall outcome of production in the end. The reason governments get involved is because of money. Certain producers of a product lobby and pay off the government to raise tariffs on imported goods so that the domestic suppliers of these goods have an advantage in selling those products to the consumers. The government sets new tariffs and thus creates one kind of monopoly for everyone involved in the process.

Essay #5

Here is another real student submission. Can you help this student by indicating revisions in the space provided? And, while you are at it, see how many words you can cut. The passage, the first three paragraphs of the essay, has 374 words in its present unpresentable form. Can you eliminate 100 More?

Do you wish to read the rest of the essay?

John Locke and the Age of Reason

In the Age of Enlightenment there was a belief of the state of reason. In fact, this is the answer as to why the Enlightenment years were called the "Age of Reason." During this time it was believed that the human nature of the people was based on reason, and that the good of human nature was there because of the people's ability to use reason to decide between right and wrong. During this "Age of Reason" Locke had a notion that because people had this ability to reason that they could live life in the state of nature. The state of nature according to Locke is "Men living together.... " (page 15, sec. 19) What this means is that people are living in a nation where there is no one to be a judge between them. Locke realizes that by not having this judge between people there would become inconveniences that would destroy the notion of the state of nature.

One of these inconveniences is that in a state of nature when a crime is done to you, you are allowed to retaliate to gain compensation for the crime. Locke believes that "it is unreasonable for men to be judges in their own cases...." (Page 14, sec. 13) He believes that when you judge your own cases your emotions get in the way and "revenge will carry too far." (Page 14, sec 13) The second inconvenience to judging your own crime, and the one that destroys the notion of this state of nature, is that once you judge your own crimes your emotions may get in the way to the point where you may convict the wrong person of doing the crime. In effect, your emotions don't allow you to gather all the facts in the case. Lastly, it is believed that when judging your own cases you may come to the point where the person who has done the crime to you is stronger than you and therefore, you cannot fight back to receive compensation for the crime that has been done to you. Due to these inconveniences in the state of nature, Locke believes there should be a government. He states, "that civil government is the proper remedy..." (Page 14, sec. 13)